Boone's Lick Road

Boone's Lick Road

A BRIEF HISTORY AND GUIDE
TO A
MISSOURI TREASURE

HAL JACKSON

FOREWORD BY KEN KAMPER

© 2012 Hal Jackson
All rights reserved. Published 2012

Jackson, Hal (Hal E.)

Boone's Lick Road, a brief history and guide
to a Missouri treasure/ Hal Jackson

ISBN 978-0-9859098-0-2

Cover illustration, chapter start illustrations
chapters one, two, four, five, six, seven
by Ron Kil

Chapter start illustration chapter three by Charlotte Plantz

Book design and type composition by Mike Plantz

This book is dedicated to
the forethought and perseverance of the
Daughters of the American Revolution
who have worked for one hundred years
to keep the memory of historic trails before the public.

Contents

Maps **viii**

Sidebars **ix**

Side Trips **ix**

Foreword **x**

Preface **xiii**

Chapter One
Early Exploration and Settlement 1

Chapter Two
Settlement in the Missouri Valley 1800 - 1815 11

Chapter Three
Franklin: Epicenter of Western Expansion 1816-1826 31

Chapter Four
St Charles City and County 41

Chapter Five
Warren & Montgomery Counties 67

Chapter Six
Callaway & Boone Counties 81

Chapter Seven
Howard County & Old Franklin 99

Maps

Boone's Lick Road/xiii
DeLisle/3
North America 1750/4
North America 1770/6
Clark's Route West/14
Femme Osage Settlements/15
Brackenridge Travels up the Missouri/17
Nathan Boone Grant/23
Principal Meridians/27
Township 48 N Range 6W/34
Population Distribution 1820/38
National Old Trails Road/40
St. Charles Historic District/42
St. Charles to Cottleville/49
Cottleville/51
Cottleville to Pond Fort/52
Soulard: Warren Cottle Grant/53
Pond Fort to Kenner's Tavern/55
Boone Settlement/58
Soulard: Boones Grants/59
Boone Home/62
Matson Area/62
Marthasville Area/63
Warren County/68
Eastern Montgomery County/70
Jonesburg/71
Danville/73
GLO Points 1816/75
Mineola/78

Williamsburg/82
West from Williamsburg/84
Auxvasse and Grand Prairie/87
Western Callaway County/88
Murry to Hinkson's Tavern/89
Brown Station to Hinton/90
West to Persia/91
Town of Persia Plat/92
Old Persia/93
Longest Segment of BLR/94
Thrall's Prairie/95
Western Boone County/98
Boonslick by Harlan/100
Salt Creek Church/104
New Franklin/105
Old Franklin/106
Old Franklin to the Lick/107
Petersburg/108
Boone's Lick Historic Site/109
Columbia to the West/113
Later Version of BLR/116

Side Trips
Boone Settlement **57**
Later Route BLR **113**

Sidebars
The Brackenridge Trip up the Missouri **16**
Surveying the Fifth Principal Meridian **25**
The Government Land Office Surveys **33**
Early Chroniclers on the Boone's Lick Road **75**
Prairie Paradox **85**
Thrall's Tavern and Lexington **96**
Old Franklin **99**
Boone's Lick **109**

Notes **117**

Bibliography **131**

Index **135**

Foreword

If you enjoy history there is nothing more interesting than an article or book that informs the reader about some important historical person or event that our history books for some reason or other never mentioned. With this book, historian-geographer Hal Jackson tells us about the most important westward migration route in America following the War of 1812, the Boone's Lick Road. This trail/road was certainly as important in its purpose as the Santa Fe, Oregon and California trails, as each had their time and purpose. The Boone's Lick Road was the earliest of the four trails, and in time was the road travelers needed to take to get to the other three. While never mentioned when we were studying history in school, the Boone's Lick Road was a trail that almost all settlers traveled from the Mississippi River to the interior of the new territory recently acquired by the United States through the Louisiana Purchase. The destination of many of those settlers was the millions of acres of rich Missouri River bottom land near the Boone Salt Lick. The word carried back east to the ears of those wanting to move west, was that the Boone's Lick region contained the most fertile land in America.

Hal Jackson not only describes the interesting history of Boone's Lick Road and the people and important events of the time, he also offers clarifying maps and describes the modern travel routes so that tourists can visit the various locations that were so well known two hundred years ago. Just think of it, two hundred years ago, the westernmost settlement of the United States was along the Boone's Lick Road. The wilderness stretched out to the north, south, and west, and the only other main route west was the Missouri River. Twenty miles west of the village of St. Charles, while along this same route in 1808, General William Clark, when stopping at a place called "Pond," wrote in his journal that he was at the westernmost white settlement. Four years earlier, as the co-leader of the Lewis and Clark Exposition, he wrote in the expedition's journals that they had arrived at a small village along the Missouri River, called Charette. The location of Charette was a dozen miles south of Pond, and it was the last white settlement that the Expedition was to see on its way to the Pacific.

The Boone's Lick Road was the main route for the vast flow of migration as America's population shifted from east of the Mississippi and headed west. In social history this upheaval of such a large segment of the population was of major historical proportions, and something that belonged in America's history books along side of the Revolutionary War and Louisiana Purchase. The Boone's Lick Road served as the main land route to populate the Missouri River valley across the state of Missouri, while also serving as the main route for persons to get to the later trails that took them to the Pacific Ocean.

The many acres of the extremely fertile Missouri River bottom land in the Boone's Lick region was well known following the Louisiana Purchase in 1803-04. However, the American government decided to survey the newly acquired land into square mile sections in order to sell and distribute the land to settlers. After a delay of eight years or so while the government fumbled its way through sorting out what to do with the land already occupied by settlers, and then another delay of three years during the War of 1812, followed by a couple of years for finally making enough surveys, the government started selling the land. Most of the land that was made available was in the region of the previous settlement west of the village of St. Louis and westward along both sides of the Missouri River to just beyond the Boone's Lick region, for a distance of about two-thirds of the way across the present state of Missouri. The effect was as though the government had set up flood gates to keep the settlers out. When the government finally opened up the land for sale, the flood gates also opened, and the mass migration of settlers from the east arrived and took to the Boone's Lick Road.

One of the least understood parts of our country's early history is this westward migration of the population from the East Coast. It was this migration of the people, for the most part, and not actions by our government, that was mostly responsible for the expansion of America all the way to the Pacific Ocean. As the people moved westward the political leadership of the country was forced to move the boundaries of their decision-making and control by treaty or otherwise, and to give political representation to the people in the new territories.

Many people started with a view of an endless wilderness to the west, with reports at times of fertile lands and abundant animals for hunting, but many others, who were mostly associated with farming, saw the west as a place of boundless opportunity. This was especially true since the word passed around in the east was that the land in the Boone's Lick region was the richest land in America. Some of the farmers who had over-cropped their farms through the years, which was indeed quite common in those days, saw the Boone's Lick region as a place to make a new start in life for themselves and their children. To go west required a set migration route that others had taken, and once it was established almost everyone followed the same road. West of the Mississippi River that road was the Boone's Lick Road.

This book tells us how a large part of America expanded west, and in doing so added some of the key components that contributed to making America the greatest country on earth. Recognition for the Boone's Lick Road is just in its infancy. An organization, "The Boone's Lick Road Association" had been forming in Missouri with the intent of getting the Boone's Lick Road recognized by Congress as one of America's "National Historic Trails." Hal Jackson's book fits well with that purpose, as it shows for the first time the importance of the road in American history. So enjoy reading some interesting history, and then take the book as your guide to find an important part of American history that America's history scholars had previously overlooked.

Ken Kamper

Boone's Lick Road

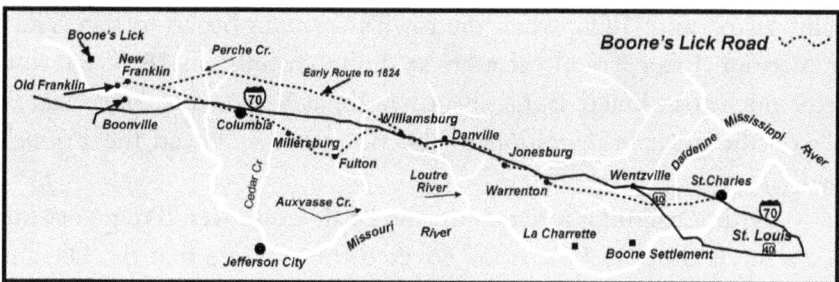

Preface

The writing of this book came about almost by accident. When I was doing field research for my book on the Santa Fe Trail (SFT) I was introduced to the late Denny Davis, who owned the newspapers in Fayette and was a recognized expert on the SFT. Denny took me under his wing and showed me the important sites and stories of the SFT in Howard County. He also made certain that I understood the importance of the Boone's Lick Road (BLR) and its connection to the SFT. When I began work on a new SFT book, I told Leo Oliva, my co-author, that we had to have a lengthy section on the BLR in the new book as it was on that road that most travelers came to Franklin and the SFT.

The Boone's Lick Road grew at each of its ends. St. Charles County, on the east, had been slowly increasing in population so that by 1812 the settlement frontier lay near the present western boundary of the county. The west, by contrast, grew because of the modest salt-working enterprise of the Boone brothers, Nathan and Daniel Morgan, at Boone's Lick. Others were attracted to the lick area, which soon gained fame as Boonslick Country.

Two things kept the two ends from growing together. First, the War of 1812 introduced great danger in Missouri so that settlers were pretty much confined to a series of forts built to protect them from Indian attacks. Second, Missouri had not been surveyed yet, so until the government surveyors completed their work, no one could buy land. Surveyors could not work as a result of Indian threats, so all had to wait until the war ended in 1815.

When the Boone's Lick Road opened in 1816 and the town of Franklin organized the same year, Franklin soon became the epicenter of rapid growth on the western frontier. Franklin's growth was dramatic and its vitality lasted until 1826, when the town's fortunes began to flag. The flooding Missouri River would eat away at the town until, in 1828, the town was pretty much abandoned. But, as historian Jonas Viles wrote, "it is clear that the bulk of the great immigration to the Boonslick followed the Boone's Lick Road."

After beginning research on the BLR, I discovered that very little had been written about it. One book covered the markers that the Daughters of the American Revolution had placed along the BLR path in 1913. Unfortunately, that book covered only the markers and the text on the markers so that one was left to imagine the rest of the story.

The BLR had another missing element. The SFT was recognized as a National Historic Trail by Congress in 1987 but, unfortunately, the BLR was not included as part of that legislation. Denny and I attempted to secure such status for the BLR in 2002, but our efforts were not successful. I can tell you now that the situation is changing. A new organization has been formed, the Boone's Lick Road Association, headed by Dave Sapp of Columbia, and this group is working hard to get National Historic Trail designation for the BLR. If they succeed, the support offered by the National Park Service to such designated trails will be invaluable.

This modest guide will provide you with background information for the period preceding the establishment of the BLR. The last four chapters are an actual guide to the roads that you can use to drive the BLR. Much of the original road, perhaps fifty per cent, is still in use. To give you an expanded view of the BLR experience, I have included eight sidebars and two side trips. Together, all of this should give you a good sense of what the BLR contributed to Missouri history.

Information for a book such as this depends on the good will and expertise of people living along the route of the BLR. These "locals" know the history of their area and are always eager to share their knowledge with others. For that reason I am indebted to the many folks along the BLR. Ken Kamper is "the" historian for Colonel Daniel Boone, Boone's family, and friends. If I have my facts straight for Boone, it is because Ken insisted I get them right.

In addition, in the St. Charles area, I thank Bob Sandfort for his careful reading and commentary on draft material I sent to him. Dorris Keeven-Franke of the St. Charles County Historical Society reviewed my section on St. Charles County. Ray Rafferty of Cottleville and Gladys Griesenhauer of Dardenne also provided valuable information on St. Charles County. I met with Steve Ehlmann in St. Charles who encouraged me to continue my BLR research. Steve wrote a book on the history of St. Charles County which proved very helpful to me.

Immediately west of St. Charles County, I relied on my good friend Ron Kamper. Ron has lived and worked in Callaway and Montgomery Counties for many years and his knowledge of the BLR in those counties is unmatched. He spent many hours driving the roads with me as I tried to make sense of the BLR in those counties. I think I have it correctly done.

Joe Crane, owner of a store and a museum in Williamsburg, is another local expert deserving my appreciation. Joe's house, which sits on the BLR in Williamsburg, is a very early log structure. In Danville I found another log house from the earliest days whose owner, Ms. Williams, allowed me to view the inside and include a photo of the inside in this volume.

The only section of the BLR that had been thoroughly researched was Boone County. David Sapp has spent years looking at every book, every scrap of information to locate the BLR and its many tavern sites and crossings. He summarized these findings in his fine book, which you will find listed in the bibliography of this volume. David is also the newly elected president of the Boone's Lick Road Association, formed in 2012.

Jim Harlan, a member of the Department of Geography at the University of Missouri in Columbia, was helpful in many ways. His superb maps of the Missouri Valley counties were invaluable as I researched the BLR. In addition, any time I needed his help on some issue I would hear his gruff voice on the phone: "You got that all wrong, Hal." He was usually right as he straightened me out.

At the Franklin end of the BLR, I can always depend on the experience and sound judgment of Mike Dickey. Mike is the administrator for the Boone's Lick Historic Site and the Arrow Rock State Park. He knows the area around Franklin intimately and was always willing to share his ideas with me.

Lastly, there are those good friends of mine I turn to for help. Ila Little did the copyediting and is a magician in turning my clumsy prose into readable English. Ila helped me with my book on the Camino Real so I knew what kind of wonderful job she would do. Mike Plantz came out of retirement to take the words, pictures, and maps and make a book out of them. The fine book you have in your hands is the result of his great work. My friends Michael and Pat Macklin steered me back on course at a critical time. Leo Oliva did much the same as I was struggling to get started on this book. Thanks to all of these friends.

I cannot forget Ron Kil, who provided the fine art work for this volume. Ron spends five hours researching a topic for every hour he spends doing the art. The cover art is truly outstanding and I think Isaac Van Bibber would approve too. Ron also drew all but one of the graphics leading off each chapter. Charlotte Plantz supplied the fine sketch of the surveyor heading Chapter Three and I thank her for that.

The maps and photos included here are mine except where noted. For the guide maps, I used US Geological Survey (USGS) maps as the base, so locations are correct.

I hope you realize that this book is a first effort. I know that much is missing and I hope others will take up the task of finding the missing parts and writing another book on the BLR. There are likely dozens of journals written by folks on their way to Oregon or California after 1840. In addition, the Mormons used the BLR on their trip to Independence in the 1830s and early 1840s.

I asked David Sapp to include a few words about the Boone's Lick Road Association and they follow with the Association's web site and address.

The Boone's Lick Road Association was recently incorporated in the State of Missouri with the express purpose of educating the public about the historic Boone's Lick Road -- the gateway land route for expansion of the United States west of the Mississippi River. The Association is also working to gain recognition of the road's importance by promoting it for the National Historic Trail program. David Sapp, President
Association web site: www.booneslickroad.org
      Mailing address: 101 South Main Street
             St. Charles, MO 63301

Chapter One
EARLY EXPLORATION AND SETTLEMENT OF THE MISSOURI VALLEY

    The Boone's Lick Road, which followed the northern ridge paralleling the Missouri River westward from St. Charles, Missouri, became an important link in a series of roads that helped open and settle the Trans-Mississippi West. Col. Daniel Boone's sons, Nathan and Daniel Morgan, began collecting salt at a salt lick in Howard County, Missouri, in 1805. The road that connected St. Charles, Missouri, and the salt lick region became known as the Boone's Lick Road. The history of the road becomes part of the story covering the development of the Mississippi-Missouri river basin, an area comprising much of North America. This region, rich in history, has received the close attention of scholars for many decades, particularly its pivotal role in the westward expansion of the United States. Before 1803 the French, and later the Spanish, dominated the political, cultural, and economic life of the basin. Then, after 1803, according to historian John Bannon, came the Americans, who "were settlers, greedy for land and seemingly insatiable in their hunger for more and more territory." Most of these explorers, traders, and settlers utilized the waters of the Missouri River Valley because almost all travel westward from the Mississippi proceeded over waterways, at least until the early nineteenth century, when Boone's Lick Road first provided some overland competition. To set the stage for that important development, I first will offer a brief history of the Mississippi-Missouri Valley and then turn to the story of the Boone's Lick Road itself.

Father Jacques Marquette and Louis Jolliet deserve credit for opening the Mississippi River basin for exploration and commerce. In 1673, with a few companions, they passed through the Straits of Michimilimackinac into Lake Michigan and followed the western shore of that lake to Green Bay, where they ascended streams from the west and then portaged to the Mississippi River drainage. From there, where Prairie du Chien would later be located, they headed south down the Mississippi, noting the river Pekitanoui (the Missouri) on their way south. The Marquette-Jolliet party was followed, in 1682, by an expedition led by René Robert Cavalier, Sieur de LaSalle, who also commented on the Missouri as "grand riviere des Emisourites," and estimated that it was navigable for 400 leagues or more.

Thus, by 1700 two French exploring parties in the Mississippi basin had reported on the Missouri River. Both parties also noted the wealth of furs that could be obtained from Indians. French fur traders would explore westward from the Mississippi Valley beginning in the mid-eighteenth century.

In 1703 Guillaume DeLisle published his first map of North America, followed by a greatly improved version in 1718 when he incorporated information given by Etienne Veniard de Bourgmont, who had traveled with some Missouri Indians up the Missouri to at least the Platte and perhaps as far as the Niobrara River. This new, revised map of 1718 was remarkably accurate and remained in use throughout the century.

Included herein is my version of DeLisle's map, in which I highlight the geographic information most relevant for this book. Note the Osage villages, located in present Saline and Lafayette counties (Missouri). To the west, De Lisle places the Apaches and Padoucas. Scholars cannot agree on who the Padoucas were. Colin Callaway writes that he thinks they were Plains Apaches or Kiowas. Some think they were Comanches, but it is hard to imagine Apaches and Comanches in the same location.

DeLisle

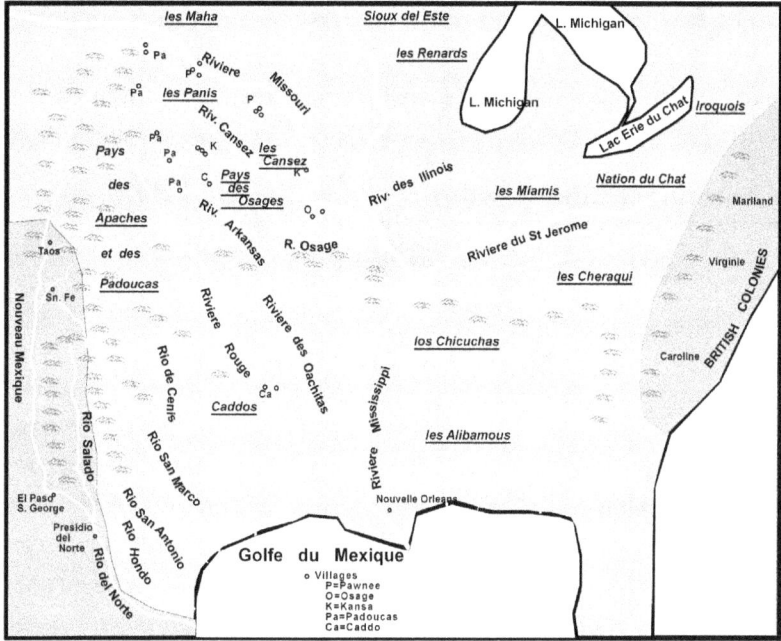

Based on a map drawn by Guillaume DeLisle in 1703. This map includes many additions and corrections based on later explorations.

Note on DeLisle's map his location of political boundaries. Neither the British nor the Spanish authorities accepted his version of claims. By 1700 Spain had pushed eastward into today's Texas in response to French intrusions in the late seventeenth century, the most important being the La Salle expedition to Matagorda Bay in 1685. The Spanish also claimed much of the Great Plains and fought to assert that claim. The British claim would have extended far west of DeLisle's line and especially to the southwest.

Chapter One
FRENCH SETTLEMENTS

The first French settlement in the Basin was at Arkansas Post in 1686, sited near the confluence of the Arkansas and Mississippi rivers. It was not a particularly good location, as the lower Arkansas was not often used to enter the interior.

North America 1750

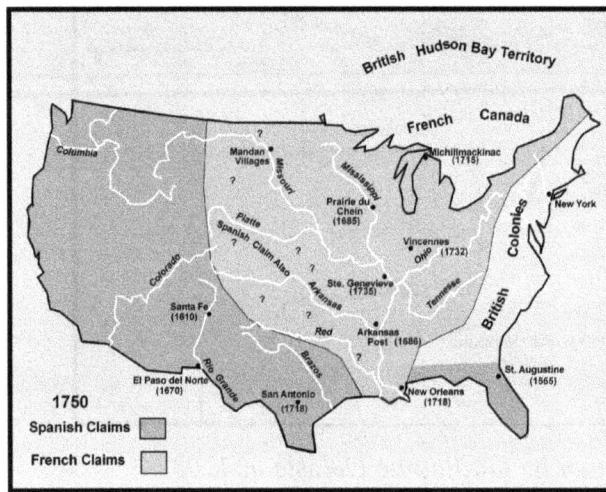

This map shows the claims of France, Spain, and Britain about 1750. Disputed territory between Spain and France is shown with question marks.

One can see from this map that several small communities and one city were established in the early decades of the eighteenth century. New Orleans, founded in 1718, became the key to French claims in the Basin, as its location near the mouth of the Mississippi River gave it control over that river, or at least the lower sections of the river. Several of the smaller communities were sited at important fords (Vincennes), river confluences (Prairie du Chien), or narrows (Michilimackinac). Fur trading with Indians was the driving economic force for their prosperity.

The most threatening event in Spain's eyes occurred in 1739, when the Mallet brothers, on a trading expedition up the Missouri, decided to go overland to New Mexico and left the Missouri River to head southwest across the Platte and Arkansas rivers. Finally, in Colorado, they met an Indian who knew the route to Santa Fe and led their party there. Thus, the Missouri became known as a jumping-off point for New Mexico.

FRENCH CONTROL IS LOST

The century-long struggle over dominance in North America between France and England ended when England won the French and Indian War (called the Seven Years War in Europe). France ceded her claims west of the Mississippi River to Spain in 1762 (also included was the Isle de Orleans to the east of the river, where New Orleans is located). The Treaty of Paris assigned French claims east of the river, including Canada, to England in 1763. With France temporarily out of the picture, what was Spain to do with this vast new territory? According to historian Abraham Nasatir, the Spanish determined to use this newly acquired territory "as a defensive barrier, or buffer, to their more valued New Spain."

From the beginning, in fact, Spain had been obsessed with protecting New Spain from foreign intrusions. Once a rich silver discovery was made near Chihuahua city in northern Mexico in the early eighteenth century, the Spanish had every reason to expect more such discoveries in the future. Fearing that other countries such as France or England might invade and occupy northern New Spain to pursue claims of their own, Spain attempted to keep all foreigners out of her territory. Even earlier, when La Salle had landed at Matagorda Bay in 1685, Spain had quickly sent an armed force to intercept the remnants of the expedition. Spanish occupation and settlement of Texas followed close behind, with the founding of San Antonio in 1718.

The other frontier of concern to Spain lay to the northeast, into the Arkansas and Missouri river country. In fact, Bourgmont's expedition in 1714 ascended the Missouri to at least the Platte, and he must have had some contact, direct or vicarious, with the Pawnees. This event became known in New Mexico by 1719 and greatly alarmed Spanish authorities.

In response, New Mexico governor Valverde in 1720 sent a substantial force under Villasur to reconnoiter the French position in Pawnee country. Somewhere on or near the Platte River in today's Nebraska, Villasur's forces were overwhelmed by the Pawnees. Only a few of its members limped back to Santa Fe to tell the story.

North America 1770

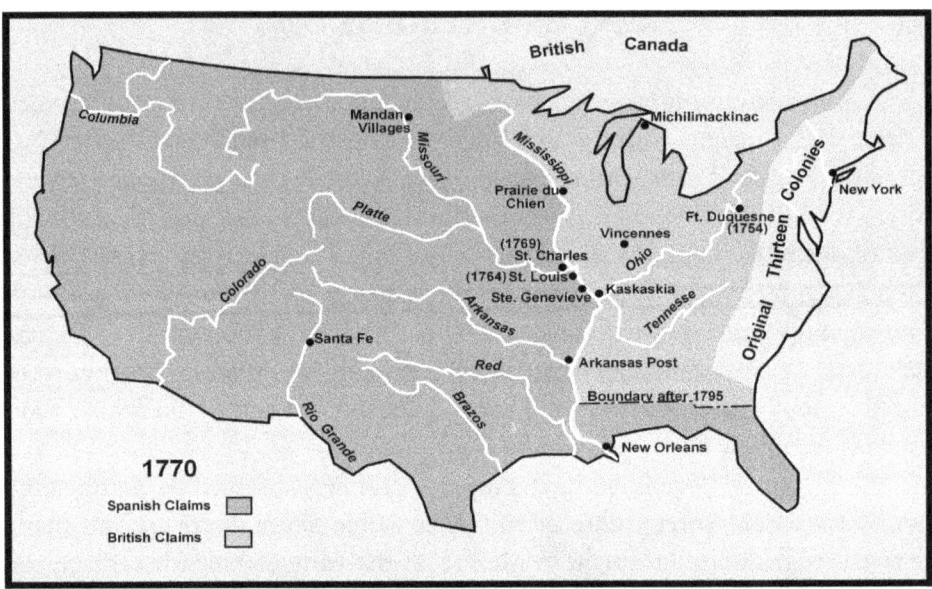

By 1770 France is out of the picture and Spain claims all land west of the Mississippi River. Note the new communities after 1750

Spanish dominion over her new eastern territory proceeded at a snail's pace. For example, Antonio de Ulloa, the first Spanish governor of Louisiana, did not arrive in New Orleans until 1766, a full two years after its acquisition from France. Historian Bannon points out that his "first experiences with these subjects in New Orleans and environs were less than pleasant." The locals, were, in fact, contentious and unwilling to assist their new masters.

Further north, the Spanish goal to control the fur trade on the Missouri River, which was the principal reason for the founding of St. Louis in 1764, met with difficulties. The British fur-trading enterprises, especially, flourished on the northern edge of the Spanish claims: Traders from the Hudson Bay area made regular appearances at the Mandan villages high up on the Missouri. Historian Nasatir summed up the problem for the Spanish as follows:

In marked contrast, the profits-starved merchants of the Spanish posts were neglected, hampered, and bound by the rigidity of their own government. Although anxious for wealth and for domination of the Indian tribes, Spain adhered to classical mercantilism. The outmoded Spanish economic system was already crushed under a great weight of taxes, poor merchandise highly priced, involved, complicated, and expensive transportation routes, a cumbersome organization, and a paternalistic hierarchy. To these ills must be added the evils of nepotism, graft, inefficiency, ignorance, and shortsightedness.

Few Spanish traders left St. Louis for the upper Missouri River country. Instead, Indians came to St. Louis seeking permission to trade with the British, according to Nasatir. He went on to write that "in a sense this represented the beginning of the end to effective Spanish control of the Upper Mississippi-Missouri region."

A few men did venture up the Missouri, like French-born Jacques d'Eglise, who, in 1790, ascended the river as far as the Mandan villages. There he discovered evidence that the English already had well-established trade links with the Mandans.

A second objective of Spain was to find migrants from Spain, France, and Germany (German Catholics of course) to settle in Louisiana. Potential emigrants in Spain, however, saw far greater economic opportunities in other parts of the Spanish Empire, from New Spain (Mexico), Peru, and other parts of Spanish South America, to the Spanish Caribbean islands, or even the Philippines.

Other than two thousand Canary Islanders enticed by cash awards, few Spaniards came to Louisiana, and even the Canary Islanders remained in New Orleans. Ironically, the greatest migration to Spanish Louisiana was French, especially the Acadians from Canada, who came by the thousands to virtually all parts of the Spanish territory.

Chapter One

AMERICANS ENTER LOUISIANA

In desperation, the Spanish finally turned to the Americans. First, in 1778, Lt. Governor Fernando de Leyba was ordered to encourage immigration into Spanish Illinois (Missouri) and treat the British and American émigrés with fairness. Nasatir wrote that by the Royal Ordinance of 1786, any who took an oath of allegiance to Spain could stay in Louisiana. When Pinckney's treaty was signed in 1795 allowing American commerce to use the Mississippi and have duty-free deposit at New Orleans, a flood of Americans began crossing the Mississippi into Upper and Lower Louisiana.

At the time of the transfer to Spain, the only community in present-day Missouri was Ste. Genevieve, a small subsistence-farming town. One immediate result of the transfer was the founding by Pierre Laclede of St. Louis in 1764, on elevated ground on the west bank of the Mississippi and very near the confluence with the Missouri River. From the beginning, St. Louis was meant to be a fur trading center and an anchor for the Spanish territorial claims on the upper Missouri River. Indians were expected to bring their furs to St. Louis to exchange for various trade goods.

The war that followed the Declaration of Independence in 1776 by the United States had an impact on Alta Louisiana (Missouri). In 1778 George Rogers Clark's forces captured Kaskaskia and Cahokia, communities on the east bank of the Mississippi. Vincennes fell later the same year. By the early 1780s, the United States controlled the entire east bank of the river.

At about the same time (1787) plans were adopted in the US Congress to survey and sell the new public lands west of the Appalachian mountain chain. The North West Ordinance went into effect in land north of the Ohio River. Because one of its provisions prohibited slavery in that territory, some early settlers who had slaves in Ohio and Indiana territory moved south of the Ohio and then west into Missouri.

Americans crossed the Appalachians into Kentucky before the conclusion of the war for independence. When it became legal after the war to move west, the movement became a flood. By 1792 Kentucky gained statehood, followed by Tennessee in 1796. Now, Spanish Missouri was looking across the river at two states and the view was not promising.

THE LAST YEARS BEFORE MISSOURI IS LOST

During the period 1785 to 1800, Spain and England were facing off in several places. Spain claimed all territory in and around the Pacific Basin because of the Treaty of Tordesillas (in which the Pope had divided the globe in two halves, Spanish and Portuguese). In North America, this meant Spain was defending the northwest coast (including Alaska) from encroachment by Russians and the English as well as its missions and presidios in coastal Alta California. In 1789 Spain and England came close to war over trading rights in the mostly insignificant Nootka Bay on what is now Vancouver Island. The issue was quickly settled, but England won substantial gains afterward. In contrast, Spain's North American claims were diminished to the 42nd parallel on the west coast (presently the northern boundary of California, Nevada, and part of Utah).

The Nootka Bay incident exemplifies the enmity between Spain and England. In our area of interest, England faced Spanish Missouri across the Mississippi until the new United States occupied Illinois and, in fact, occupied some parts of the Northwest Territory, as the Americans called it, until the conclusion of the War of 1812.

As I noted earlier, England had developed a "complete monopoly of Indian trade on both sides of the Mississippi north of St. Louis." To make matters worse for Spain, St. Louis merchants were buying their goods through Montreal instead of New Orleans largely because the British buyers paid higher prices for peltries. However, most of the merchandise for Missouri was brought to Cahokia from Michilimackinac.

This period is noted for the influx of opportunistic Americans seeking to take advantage of a weakened Spain. One such man was James Wilkinson, called by Nasatir "the greatest of all intriguers." Others called him a villain and a scoundrel. Wilkinson served in the Revolutionary War with some distinction and went on to various ventures in the American Mississippi and Louisiana areas. In 1787 he went to New Orleans where he met with the Spanish governor. From 1790 on, he maintained secret contacts with the Spanish authorities. Even while he was involved with Aaron Burr in 1804 and 1805, finally turning on him and testifying against him at his treason trial, and despite being appointed by President Jefferson as the first governor of Northern Louisiana in 1805 and serving until 1807, Wilkinson remained on the payroll of Spain the entire time regularly contacting Spanish officials about American plans.

Thus, Missouri, in 1790, was relatively secure for Spain. Still, across the Mississippi River lay American territory, which would become the states of Kentucky and Tennessee, and further down the Mississippi, in Baja Louisiana, Spain and the United States were arguing about which country owned the east bank. Finally, Pinckney's Treaty in 1795 established 31 degrees north latitude as the international boundary. The treaty also opened the Mississippi to American shipping. And in Alta Louisiana, north of Missouri, England was the master of all.

One additional threat facing Spain came from a group of men called filibusters. William Blount, in 1797, concocted a plan to conquer three Spanish towns including New Madrid. A second and better-known scheme by Philip Nolan involved entering eastern Texas and taking it over. Nolan's plot failed when the Spanish learned about it (perhaps from James Wilkinson) and killed Nolan in Texas.

By 1800, Missouri included several distinct communities. The oldest, Ste. Genevieve, was established before Louisiana became Spanish and had a population of almost one thousand. St. Louis was next in population with about 900; San Carlos (St. Charles) had 800 or so. New Madrid, in southern Missouri, had almost 800 residents. Most importantly for our purposes, the Boone Settlement was established southwest of St. Charles and a few miles downriver from La Charrette, the most distant community on the Missouri River at this time.

Chapter Two
SETTLEMENT IN THE MISSOURI VALLEY 1800 TO 1815

The first two decades of the nineteenth century proved to be interesting and challenging for residents of the lower Missouri River valley who were concerned primarily with land issues: who owned which parcel, and how someone else could obtain it. Spain's sovereignty was quickly followed by French and then American control. To complicate matters, while France technically owned Upper Louisiana, its governance remained in the hands of Spaniards. How legal were those land grants made by the Spanish after France became owner? That question would be left for American courts and officials to decide.

In 1804, the year the United States assumed control of Louisiana, the entire District of St. Charles had a population of about 1400 whites and perhaps 150 Negro slaves. The extended Boone family was a significant part of the American contingent here in 1804. Col. Daniel Boone had arrived in late 1799, responding to an invitation to settle by the Spanish Governor Trudeau. Accompanying Boone was his extended family of Callaways, Van Bibbers,

Hays, and others. They chose land in the general vicinity of Daniel Morgan Boone's earlier obtained (1797) Spanish grant near the confluence of Femme Osage Creek and the Missouri River (Matson today). Thus began the very important Boone Settlement, a term mentioned by one of Lewis and Clark's men in his journal.

Historian Jonas Viles estimated that three-fifths of the residents of the District of St. Charles were Americans. Many of them crossed over into Missouri after 1800 when the political situation was in flux and when Spanish attitudes toward Americans had softened, making land grants easier to obtain. Then there were the land speculators who came to Missouri to make their fortune buying up land concessions.

Most settlers were subsistence hunters and farmers who shot game or grew their own food, made their own clothes, and built their homes. Of course they could not provide some essential products. Salt, for example, was very important for them as it was used to tan leather and preserve meat. Gunpowder and shot were also in demand. There was, then, some modest trade taking place.

Settlement adjacent to the small town of St. Charles began even before the American takeover in 1804. During the first ten years of the nineteenth century, the population of the lower Missouri valley grew slowly but steadily. The newcomers were mostly Americans from Kentucky and Virginia. A few settlers came from Europe but these, too, had made a stop in Pennsylvania, Maryland, or Kentucky. Mostly subsistence farmers but still needing some access to markets, the newcomers settled along the Missouri River or adjacent to St. Charles.

In this writer's opinion, the migration of Col. Daniel Boone's family into Missouri in 1799 and 1800 played a large part in attracting other Americans to Missouri. It was sort of "what's good for Col. Boone is good for me." But whereas Boone had received a grant of land from the Spanish, many latecomers were not so fortunate because the United States government made no public land available in Missouri until 1818. Yet these new settlers were coming to Missouri, where they could not buy public land, while passing through Ohio, Indiana, Illinois, and Kentucky, which offered hundreds of thousands of surplus acres to them.

In 1800 St. Charles and its immediate environs were the only settled area north of the Missouri River except for Charrette, a very small collection of French families constituting a village a few miles upstream from St. Charles on the Missouri. From St. Charles, a few families moved west onto or near the future Boone's Lick Road. John Kountz (or Countz), for example, first lived in St. Charles, where he bought land from the town's founder, Louis Blanchette, and built a new gristmill on Blanchette Creek upstream from the Blanchette mill in the 1790s. Then, in 1800, Kountz moved to a land grant six miles west of town on Dardenne Creek, where he built two more mills, according to historian Kate Gregg.

The earliest landowners in St. Charles County came from a multitude of places. There were, of course, the many French from Quebec who came here very early, like Louis Blanchette. Others, the Kountzes (John and Nicholas) and the Zumwalts and the Hoffmans, were originally from Germany and came by way of Pennsylvania, Maryland, or Kentucky. George Spencer, an early recipient of a grant, came from England. The Cottles, three of them, migrated from Vermont while the Baldridges arrived from Ireland. Lastly, Arend Rutgers, owner of the largest grant, came from Holland.

By 1803 several gristmills were working on the Dardenne beyond those of John Coontz. Where there are mills, farmers congregate and socialize. These mills thus became the nucleus of a small hamlet near the ford of the Dardenne where Cottleville lies today, making it the first community to be established west of St. Charles.

Farmers who brought their wheat and corn to be ground at gristmills paid for the milling by giving part of the flour to the miller, a practice that led to a small surplus of flour. To move the surplus flour to the closest market, which was St. Charles, a farm-to-market road developed between the Dardenne and St. Charles, becoming by 1815 part of the road that led to Boone's Lick Country, centered on Franklin in Howard County.

Gregg was writing about the Boone's Lick Road when she said, "it was rather the expression of a road tendency than confinement of travel to a single described route." Individual landowners petitioned the county to adopt "their" road and abandon someone else's road. There was no single road, especially when one traveled beyond the Dardenne at Cottleville, where routes variously continued on the divide separating Dardenne and Peruque Creeks.

Clark's Route West

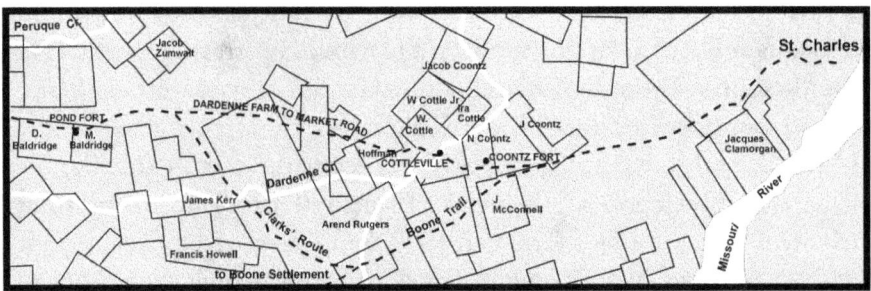

This map shows the approximate route that William Clark followed from St. Charles to the west in 1808. His guide was Nathan Boone and Boone chose not to take the usual route through Cottleville but instead take a route farther south crossing smaller creeks tributary to the Dardenne.

The first organized trip west from St. Charles occurred in 1808 when William Clark with eighty men headed for western Missouri to establish a trading fort. Guide for the expedition was Nathan Boone. The exact route is unclear, but it almost certainly followed the Boone Trail (called the Marthasville Road after 1820) to at least John Howell's grant. From there it continued west to "a Pond at the out Skirts of the Settlement in a beautiful Plain, near a few low trees." With these words Clark identified what must have been a pond on Milciah Baldridge's grant eight miles west of today's Cottleville. Boone was leading his charge toward a ridge that followed the divide between creeks draining into the Mississippi and Missouri Rivers. To be clear, the first divide separated the Dardenne and Peruque Creeks, both of which flow into the Mississippi. Once across Dardenne Creek, the path led westward between streams draining into the Mississippi and Missouri Rivers. Clark's route became known as the Osage Trail, and the later Boone's Lick Road followed much of its course to Franklin.

To summarize then, farmers living on Spanish grants west of St. Charles to within a few miles of the present Warren County line were anxious to have the county provide farm-to-market roads so they could gain access to the St. Charles market and, by extension, the St. Louis market. The road west left St. Charles at the Chouteau mill site, climbed the hill and turned west on the Boone Trail to about John Howell's grant, where it continued due west and headed to the ford of the Dardenne at Cottleville. From that point, several competing roads all headed to the Pond Fort area (simply the Milciah Baldridge grant at the time), including the one later to be known as the Boone's Lick Road.

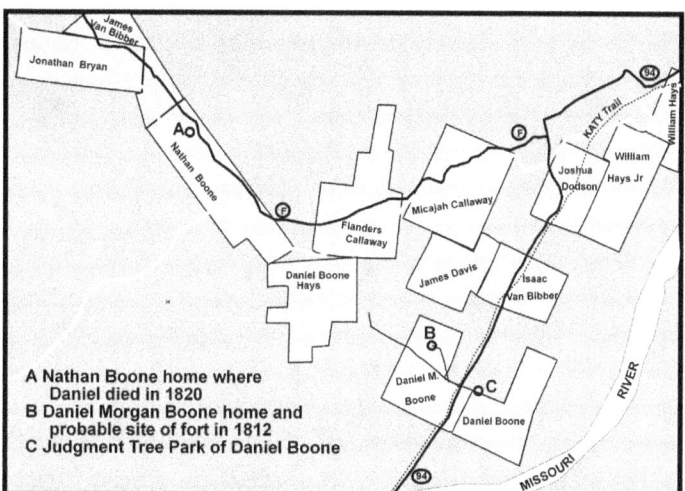

The early Boone Settlement along the Femme Osage and Missouri River.

On the included map, one can see the general distribution of the "Boone" settlers. Several, including Nathan Boone, who had to buy his grant, were scattered along Femme Osage Creek. Daniel Boone took his 1000-arpent (845 acres) grant adjacent to that of his son Daniel Morgan Boone. The clan would eventually own land from Femme Osage Creek on the Missouri bottoms as far as Charrette (near the later Marthasville).

Our best reporter, H. M. Brackenridge, found scattered plantations along the river bottoms when he ascended the river by keelboat in 1811. In addition to the Boone Settlement, he found congregated settlements at Cote san Dessein (twenty French families) and Loutre Island. By far the largest and most prosperous settlement was in present Howard County, across from the mouth of the Lamine River. Benjamin Cooper and his family moved to this location in 1808 but were ordered back by Governor Meriwether Lewis because the Indian titles were not yet extinguished. Cooper then went downriver to Loutre Island, remaining there two years before returning to the

Howard County area, where he settled about two miles southwest of a salt lick begun by the Boone brothers, Nathan and Daniel Morgan, in 1806. Hannah Cole and her nine children and brother-in-law Stephen Cole settled across the river in today's Boonville. The Boone brothers, Nathan and Daniel Morgan, made salt at the nearby salt spring starting in 1806 and their efforts led to the name Boone's Lick being applied to the area around the salt springs. In 1811 there were about seventy-five families here, according to Henry Brackenridge. The entire area soon became known as Boonslick Country.

The Brackenridge Trip up the Missouri in 1811

Henry Brackenridge's *Journal of a Voyage Up the Missouri River In 1811* provides us with a wealth of valuable and entertaining information. The author tells us that what he recorded was simply "hasty notes" but, in fact, we discover how traders and others ascended the Missouri in the early pre-steamboat era. We learn how the crew managed to ascend the river with a twenty-ton keelboat, against a steady current, and go from St. Charles to the Boone's Lick settlement in only twelve days. Two hundred miles upstream in twelve days meant that the crew averaged about seventeen miles per day.

Brackenridge's journal is important because it fills an important gap in the history of the early nineteenth-century Missouri river valley. Lewis and Clark in 1804 and Pike in 1806 describe the valley for us, but the next well-known visitor to write about it was Stephen Long in 1819. Brackenridge's journal captures the rapid changes taking place in the years immediately prior to the War of 1812-1815. For that reason, his journal deserves to be remembered.

Mr. Brackenridge, a lawyer by profession and the son of an important lawyer in Pennsylvania, was in St. Louis apparently on a vacation of sorts, as we are never told what business he might have had in that city.

While there he met Manuel Lisa of the Missouri Fur Company, who invited Brackenridge to accompany him upriver where Lisa would be trading with various Indian tribes for furs. On a lark Brackenridge accepted the offer and on Tuesday, April 2, 1811, the expedition left St. Charles in one keelboat.

Lisa was attempting to overtake another trading expedition led by Wilson

Brackenridge's Travels up the Missouri

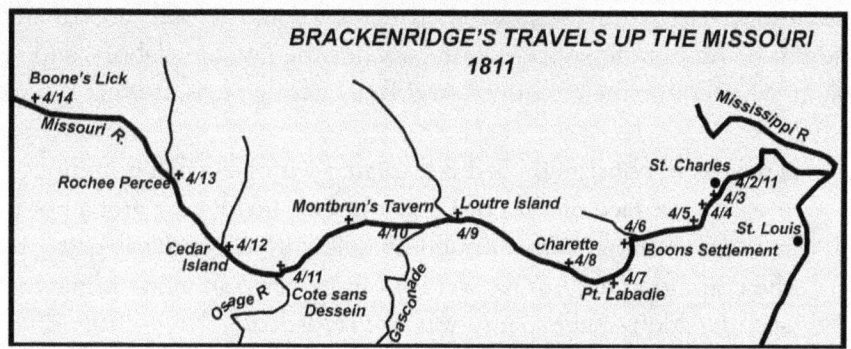

The map shows Brackenridge's progress up the Missouri in 1811, Except for the first few days, Brackenridge made good time.

Hunt, who served the Astor group. It was important to make up Hunt's twenty-one day head start as Lisa hoped to join the Hunt party so that the combined forces could better protect the traders from possible Indian depredations.

According to Brackenridge, the boat "proceeded a few miles above St. Charles, we put to shore, some of our men still remaining at the village." The crew consisted of twenty men, of which a few had made at least one prior trip upriver. Passengers included Manuel Lisa, Brackenridge, and the patron (the sailing master in charge of the crew), as well as a "Frenchman named Charbonet, with his wife, an Indian woman of the Snake nation, both of whom had accompanied Lewis and Clark to the Pacific."

They traveled but a few miles that first day. "It is exceedingly difficult to make a start on these voyages," Brackenridge tells us, because of "the reluctance of the men to terminate the frolic with their friends, which usually preceded their departure." They would drink and carouse, making it almost impossible to collect them on board. Many owed a tavern owner a bar bill and the tavern owners knew "that their employer will be compelled to pay." Thus, the boat traveled but a few miles the first day while Lisa remained in St. Charles collecting the truant men and paying their bar bills. Even the second day was a problem, as they did not depart until after two o'clock and made but six miles.

The crew consisted of Canadians and creoles, according to Brackenridge. He greatly admired their dexterity and wrote, "an American could not be brought to support with patience the fatiguing labors, and submission, which these men endure." And Brackenridge tells us what the crew was fed:

> Their food consists of lied [i.e. treated with lye] corn hominy for breakfast, a slice of fat pork and a biscuit for dinner, and a pot of mush for supper, with a pound of tallow in it. Yet this is better than the common fare; but we were about to make an extraordinary voyage, the additional expense was not regarded.

Reading Brackenridge's concluding comment that the additional expense was appropriate for the "extraordinary voyage," one can only imagine what a crew was fed on an ordinary voyage.

Lisa had outfitted the keelboat with a good mast and rigging in order to utilize favorable winds. From the journal it is clear that wind power was used a great deal, especially in mornings. They were constantly switching from bank to bank as the river meandered back and forth. Oars were used at times, as were poles if the water was not too deep. Cleats would have been attached to the deck to assist the crew's footing. When all else failed, the crew would jump in the river and tow the boat. Perhaps grappling hooks would be used to help pull the boat through rough stretches.

Reading the journal, one feels the dramatic changes occurring along the river as the boat goes higher and higher up the Missouri. Numerous farms, called plantations at the time, are noted. Even a few communities are mentioned. On the fifth day, April 6th, the boat was forced to stop because of high winds blowing "directly down the river." "This is near Boon's settlement," Brackenridge notes. This settlement was a collection of farms and houses stretching from present-day Defiance in St. Charles County to

Marthasville in Warren County.

On the 7th of April the party passed Point Labadie on the southwest side. Brackenridge notes that they only made fourteen miles that day and explains that they were slowed as a result of obstruction by several embaras. These were literally "rafts formed by a collection of trees closely matted, and extending from twenty to thirty yards." The crew were forced to use grappling hooks and when that did not work, the towing line with the crew in the water made for a very dangerous situation if the boat should swing around.

He notes that in the bends of the river the banks would sometime fall in and trees would stand out in the river itself. In locations such as these, where the water was too deep for poling, the crew pulled the boat along with their hands tree to tree.

On the 8th they reached the little village of Charette. When Lewis and Clark passed here in 1804 and Zebulon Pike in 1806, Charette was the last settlement on the river. By now, about thirty families lived here, hunting and raising corn. Upstream from Charette the boat passed high bluffs on the southwest side, where Brackenridge locates Isle aux Boeufs. This island is noted on modern maps, but the Missouri river has shifted course and now runs south of the island instead of north.

Tuesday, the 9th, he writes, "we set off this morning with a light breeze, which continued to augment until ten, when from a change in the course of the river, it was unfavorable for two or three miles." He noted several plantations on both sides and the compact settlement on the isle a la Loutre. This settlement lay on the western end of Loutre Island and a bit upstream from the present Warren-Montgomery county line. At four o'clock the same day the boat passed the mouth of the Gasconade river. They were able to use their sails that afternoon and made six miles above the Gasconade.

Next morning they crossed to the northeast side and passed "Montbrun's tavern and river." This was a very high rock bluff where protection was available for travelers in inclement weather; it is located near the mouth of Little Tavern creek in southeast Callaway County. Brackenridge writes, "from the color of the water on the S. W. side, it appears that the Osage river is paying its annual tribute."

Our author reached Cote sans Dessein by foot, having deserted the boat for a two-mile walk to this small village, almost a replica of Charette, passed several days earlier. "The Cote sans Dessein, is a beautiful place, situated on the N. E. side of the river, and in sight of the Osage. It will in time become a considerable village." There were thirteen families here when he visited, hunting for the most part with a little farming.

As a result of favorable winds and few obstacles, the boat made twenty-eight miles on the 13th of April, and they camped near Roche persee (pierced rock). Brackenridge writes that their good fortune on this day may have been reward for a good deed performed the previous day when they spent an hour helping an ox trapped in sand near the shore:

> The poor creature had remained here ten or twelve days, and the sand into which he had sunk, was become hard and solid. The wolves had paid him friendly visits from time to time, to inquire after his health, while buzzards, crows, and eagles, tendered their salutations from the boughs of the neighboring trees.

The boat was passing the Mine river (Lamine river in Cooper County) on the southwest side on a Sunday and Brackenridge comments on the numerous salt works on that river. Across the Missouri, on the northeast, stood a flourishing settlement whose residents came out in their Sunday best to greet the boat. This, of course, was the Boone's Lick community. He said it had been here but one year and was growing very rapidly. He stopped at the farm of Braxton Cooper, who was manager of the salt works at the nearby Boone's Lick. The settlement had seventy-five families spread along the banks of the river for four or five miles. Cooper told him that from the mouth of the Missouri to this point the upland areas (area bordering the river) for at least forty miles from the river was good land for settlement, mostly woodland with but a "trifling proportion" of prairie. At that time most people felt that woodlands made good farm land and prairies did not.

The keelboat continued its journey up the Missouri, reaching Fort Osage on Tuesday, April 25th. Brackenridge describes the fort as being "handsomely situated, about one hundred feet above the level of the river." He adds, "The fort is small, not calculated for more than a company of men." There were sixty lodges of the Little Osages very close to the fort and recently many bands of Osages along with some Kansas Indians had visited the fort to trade.

Still chasing Hunt's two boats, the Lisa party passed the Kansas river on 28 April. On the 29th, they made thirty miles because of favorable winds. Finally, on May 10 they found themselves a little upstream from the mouth of the Platte and in open country. The Platte, according to Brackenridge, was the "equinoctial line" for Missouri river travelers: those on board who had not passed the Platte before "were required to be shaved, unless they could compensate the matter by a treat."

Finally, on June 2nd, Brackenridge sighted the boats of the Hunt party and that afternoon was re-united with a friend of his, the naturalist John Bradbury, who was traveling with Hunt. From this point Brackenridge describes meeting with various Indian parties and warns that "the lovers of Indian manners, and mode of living, should contemplate them at a distance." Cleanliness, apparently, was not considered a virtue among the Indians he visited.

They reached the Mandan villages and company fort on Wednesday, June 26. This was, according to Brackenridge, 1440 miles from the mouth of the Missouri. On the sixth day of July, Brackenridge was placed in charge of two boats filled with furs and directed to take the boats and cargo back to St. Louis as fast as he could. They arrived at St. Louis in early August, making the 1440-mile trip in only fourteen days.

LAND PROBLEMS

When Upper Louisiana became part of the young United States on March 10, 1804, the amount of territory in this transfer was yet to be determined, but there were approximately ten thousand people (not including Indians) in the acquisition. As I have suggested, the question of land ownership would dominate the territory until 1818, when public lands would finally go on sale. John Thomas wrote, "From March 10, 1804, to that day [August 3, 1818] no one had been able to obtain, by purchase or gift, title to any of the public lands for home making, or for speculation." Indeed, an act of 1804 imposed fines or imprisonment for unauthorized surveying and settling, and this act remained in force until 1818.

The period between the purchase in 1803 and the transfer of authority in 1804 was one of transition. The words in the cession resonated: "The inhabitants...shall be maintained in the full enjoyment of their property." To many settlers these words meant the United States would accept their claims to land. Others, convinced their concessions were worthless, sold them for almost nothing.

It is beyond the scope of this book to detail all the shenanigans that went on during these early years of the century. Lamont Richardson's three-part article "Private Land Claims in Missouri" should be consulted for these details. I will mention here only a few of the speculators known to have bought concessions, forged documents, and manipulated government officials. They include Rufus Easton, Jacques St. Vrain, Louis Labeaume, Charles Gratiot, Auguste Chouteau, Sr., James Mackay, and Jacques Clamorgan. It should be mentioned that our friend Gen. James Wilkinson, who governed during the period 1805-1807, was courted by one side and then the other, and continued to distinguish himself as a scoundrel.

The only way that one of the hordes of Americans flocking to Missouri could obtain land was to buy someone else's confirmed concession. Pre-emption, a method commonly used to obtain land farther east, was not allowed in the beginning. Pre-emption was a system whereby one occupied some land so that when it became open for sale, one had first rights to buy it. Finally, in 1814, pre-emption was allowed but only for those inhabiting land before 1814. After the New Madrid earthquakes occurred in 1812 and 1813, the federal government, by an Act of Congress, issued certificates to those whose land had been destroyed. These certificates, which allowed the holders to claim open government-owned land, became almost legal tender and were sold and resold. Many were used to claim land in Missouri late in the period 1815 to 1820.

The Spanish, and later the Americans, had the same philosophy for land distribution. First, grants should go to bona fide settlers on small tracts.

SETTLEMENT IN THE MISSOURI VALLEY

Second, in the case of American land distribution, cash sales were a source of revenue for the government. Third, the land was supposed to be sufficient to support a man and his family. Farms at the time were subsistence for the most part, and a few hundred acres was more than enough for crops and a tract of woods for firewood and home building.

The government-appointed board that investigated claims for possible confirmation looked at 3000 claims and confirmed 1342. About one-third of these were confirmed by 1812. Many more were later confirmed by court action. The site of the actual "Boone's Lick" in Howard County was part of a

Soulard Map

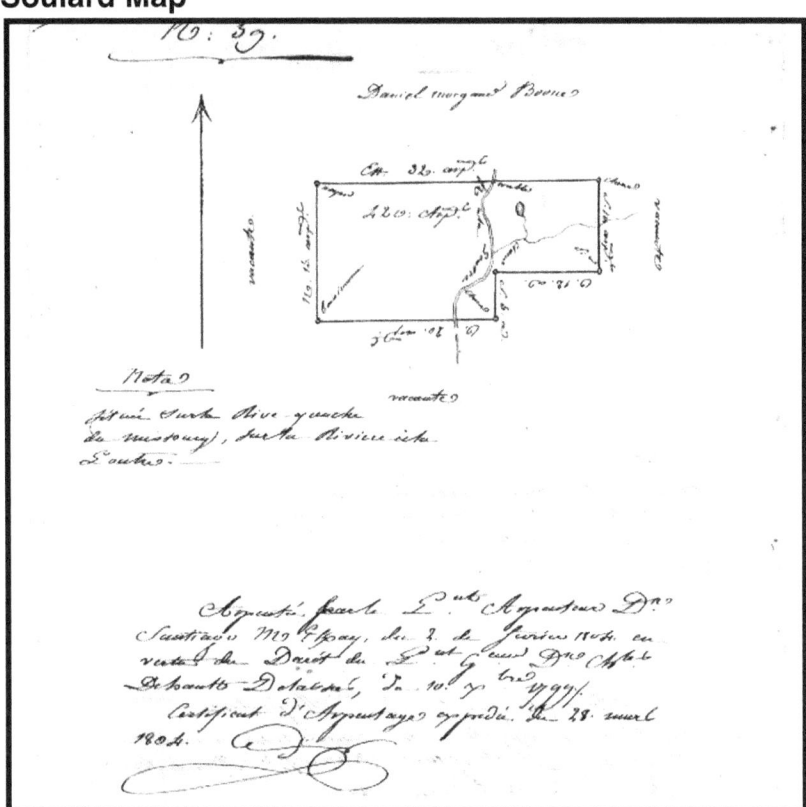

Nathan Boone's grant straddles the Loutre River. The map shows the salt spring as well as two fords, one near the spring, the other on the Loutre itself. Isaac Van Bibber would build his famous tavern near the salt spring. Courtesy of the Missouri State Archives.

claim made by James Mackay, whose grant was not confirmed until 1835, long after Mackay's death.

Antoine Soulard, who had been Surveyor General under the last two Spanish Lt. Governors and then retained by the Americans, produced many fine tract maps. I have included three of Soulard's maps for you to see and admire (one in the Side Trip to the Boone Settlement and another in Chap. 3, and the one here). The early Spanish grants were distributed mainly along the Missouri River, from St. Charles to Howard County. They are a patchwork of claims with a variety of shapes. One distinguishing feature of the early grants is that they are rarely oriented north-south and are usually irregular in shape, as though the older metes and bounds system was in play. Both the Clark and Femme Osage maps presented earlier in this chapter show the variety of shapes and orientation of the grants.

A modern reader may certainly want to know why it took from 1804 until 1818 for the United States government to begin land sales in Missouri. Many folks in Missouri at the time also wanted to know. Some possible explanations for the delay include these:

1. The Spanish land grant issue had to be resolved first. Legitimate claimants had to know their land was safe from claims by other settlers. By 1812, this issue was fairly well resolved.
2. Indian claims had to be cleared. The Osages who lived south of the Missouri and west of the Gasconade River and the Sauk, Fox, and Iowa Indians in northern Missouri had valid claims and all these had to be taken care of as well.
3. The War of 1812 was especially hard-fought in Missouri. Indians attacked settlements and farmsteads throughout the territory. In addition, the war in Missouri did not end with the signing of the Peace Treaty in December 1814. The Indians continued their attacks until well into the summer of 1815. When treaties were finally signed with the Indians after peace talks were held at Portage des Sioux in July 1815, much land was freed up.
4. The United States had adopted a system in 1787 to be used in surveying newly won territory. The first such surveys were made along the Ohio River and west of Pennsylvania soon after. The first step was to determine a start-

ing point and from that point survey base lines and a principal meridian. (A later sidebar will explain this process.) For Missouri, the chosen starting point was where the Arkansas and Mississippi Rivers come together. The survey of this north line, the Fifth Principal Meridian, began October 27, 1815, and was completed May 26, 1816. After the meridian was established, townships and sections had to be surveyed. All of this was work completed into Howard County by 1818, a really remarkable achievement for such a short time. (There are now (2012) thirty-seven principal meridians in the US.)

5. The United States government did not feel the need to expedite the Missouri surveys since there was already more than enough land surveyed and available in Indiana and Illinois for settlers.

Still, thousands of settlers came to the new Eden of Missouri and wanted land. Finally, and despite delays caused by the complications I have just mentioned, in November of 1818 a land office opened for business in Franklin, Howard County.

Surveying the Fifth Principal Meridian

Settlement in Missouri depended on several issues. First, Indian titles to vast tracts of land had to be extinguished. This issue with the Osages had been mostly cleared by 1808. The Sauk and Fox claims had to wait until the conclusion of hostilities in the War of 1812. These were extinguished beginning in 1815.

The second issue dealt with the surveying of the public lands. The ordinance that spelled out the system of surveys to be used in our country's new lands passed Congress May 20, 1785. The story behind the adoption of the new survey system is an interesting one.

Thomas Jefferson chaired the committee that Congress appointed to devise a survey system. The committee reported in

May 1784 that the lands were to be divided into tracts ten miles square and these tracts into lots one mile square, giving 100 lots numbered 1 to 100. That ordinance was amended in 1785 and this time the townships, as they were now called, were to be seven miles square and have forty-nine sections. The ordinance was amended yet again May 20, 1785, so that townships should be six miles square, divided into thirty-six sections. This system, as most know, is what is used today.

I said the story was an interesting one and what makes it so is Jefferson and the first system the committee suggested. Payson Treat wrote that even though "the report was in Jefferson's handwriting yet one can hardly infer that he 'invented' the system which was outlined." Jefferson had an extensive library and was a very well read person. He may have known that the Romans devised a land survey system for their newly conquered lands. Called "centuriation," it too was based on one hundred, had parallel demarcation lines with others at right angles. One can still see on maps and air photos of northern Italy this land use pattern. It has persisted, as will ours I think, through two thousand years of use. The one difference between Roman and the US adoption was our requirement that dividing lines be precisely north-south and east-west. The Roman system is turned a bit to the east.

The system we use requires that a standard meridian, a north to south line, be surveyed followed by a base line running east to west. The intersection of the meridian and base line is a point, a place from which surveys refer. In the case of Missouri, the meridian (the Fifth Principal Meridian) was to begin at the confluence of the Mississippi and Arkansas Rivers. The base line for the Missouri surveys ran through the mouth of the St. Francis River.

The work of surveying the Fifth Principal Meridian began October 27, 1815. The surveyors reached the Missouri River on December 28, 1815, without passing through a single settlement. The work on the northern part of the Meridian began January 1, 1816, and reached the northern line of Township 50 on January 31,

1816. This unique and important line is easy to find in our area of interest, as it is the western boundary of St. Charles County.

Principal Meridians and Baselines in Mississippi Valley

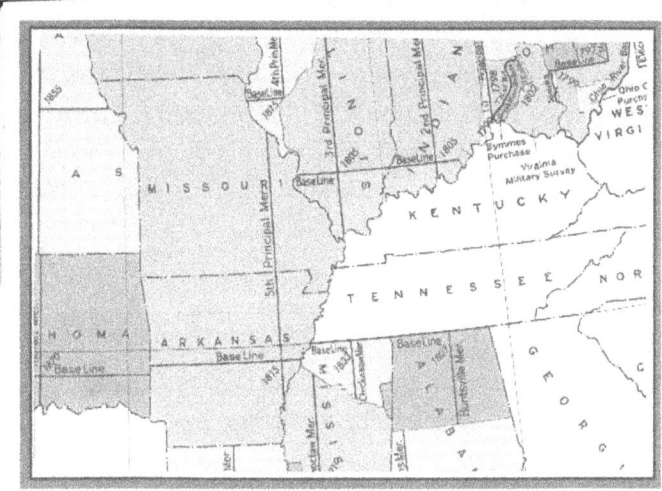

Map from Bureau of Land Management and shows the many meridians and baselines in and around Missouri.

Completing the Principal Meridian was only part of the job. Now, in May 1816, surveyors began marking range, township, and section lines. It took more than two years, until the middle of 1818, to complete the surveys and make the territory ready for land sales. Sales began at St. Louis August 3, 1818, with the price set at $2 an acre, one twentieth in cash and the balance in five annual installments. Sales at Franklin were delayed until November 2, 1818. According to Thomas, the credit system outlined above proved disastrous, "and in 1820, Congress interposed for the relief of those who had gone in debt beyond their means to pay, and the price of lands was reduced to $1.25 an acre in cash."

War of 1812

Before we move on, a few words may be in order to clarify the impact on Missouri's inhabitants of the War of 1812, for few of us are familiar with the details of how that conflict was fought in the western territories. In Missouri, Indians from the north who were supported by England invaded the territory of the Osage Indians, which was protected by a treaty signed in 1802 by William Clark on behalf of the U S government. For Missouri territory, the war began in 1811 and did not end before 1815 or even 1816. Gregg covers the bloody details in her three-part article "The War of 1812 on the Missouri Frontier."

In an attempt to protect settlers and their families from Indian invasions from the north, the Government established several companies of U S Rangers, and the settlers took refuge in one of the many forts constructed early in the war. Even the simple act of plowing one's field required someone to stand guard and warn of potential danger from Indians. Thus the settlement frontier between 1811 and 1816 was static, or perhaps it even retreated. Even Fort Osage, far to the west and reasonably well protected, was closed in June 1813. To meet U S treaty obligations of 1808 with the Osages, a factory (trading post) was opened at Arrow Rock in late December 1813. It contained a two-story blockhouse 30 by 20 feet in dimension, which was also forced to close, in 1814.

Cooper's Fort

Sketch of Cooper's Fort in Howard County about 1813. The palisades are too high in the sketch but it still shows the basic plan of a fort. Courtesy of the artist Stephanie Witte.

Forts were established within a few miles of St. Charles as refuge for settlers in what is now St. Charles County, including Kountz Fort, Pond Fort, Castlio's Fort, Kennedy's Fort, and, Daniel Morgan Boone's fort. Three forts, including Cooper's Fort, one of the largest, were established near the salt works in Howard County. All these forts became targets for attacking Sauk and Fox Indians, and their allied tribes (Miami, Winnebago, Pottawattamie, and Kickapoos). Sarshall Cooper was killed in his own house within the walls of Cooper's Fort in April 1814.

Chapter Three
Franklin: Epicenter of Western Expansion
1816-1826

Kate Gregg writes that after the Treaty of Ghent was signed December 24, 1814, "news of the peace arrived too early" as there "had been no smashing defeat of the Indians." She continues, "in the opinion of the frontier, Indians yielded to no argument but that of force." Her claims are illustrated by the fact that during the interval between the signing of the Treaty of Ghent and the initiation of negotiations with the Indians at Portage des Sioux (July 1815), Indians launched major attacks on Cotes sans Dessein, Loutre Island, the Boonslick country, and the Femme Osage area. On March 7, 1815, Captain James Callaway and four others were killed on the Loutre. In addition, in an event that especially shocked the settlers, the Ramsey family was murdered near Charrette on May 20, 1815. Not until June of 1816 did the last of the ten tribes who failed to appear at the Portage des Sioux negotiations sign a treaty. Only then, Dr. Gregg writes, was the "path of western emigration… theoretically open."

Nevertheless, even during these dangerous times there was still some commerce and travel from St. Charles to the Boone's Lick Country. It was too dangerous to make that journey by horseback but the Missouri River still was reasonably safe. Raymond Thomas called the Missouri River the "highway into the interior." Keelboats would bring necessary supplies for the salt works upriver and take salt and other commodities down to the settlements along the river, as well as to St. Louis. There was also the earlier main westward route along the north bank of the Missouri called Boone's Trace, but it was not useable for wagons. In 1816 the population in the valley lived very close to St. Charles or on the shores of the Missouri River.

BOONE'S LICK ROAD

I am sorry to tell you that we are unlikely to find a William Becknell or a Juan de Oñate who championed the opening of the Boone's Lick Road (BLR). (Becknell is the well-known pioneer on the Santa Fe Trail (SFT), opened in 1821, while Oñate led the first settlers into New Mexico along the Camino Real in 1598.) First, we must understand that we are talking about a road, a route that was used by wagons and other wheeled vehicles. William Clark, guided by Nathan Boone, traveled by horse from St. Charles to the Boone's Lick Country in 1808, but he had no wheeled vehicles in his entourage.

I rely on evidence in the Government Land Office (GLO) surveys of 1816 through 1818 in this part of Missouri to support my position on the opening of the BLR. Skilled surveyors walked every section line noting all the creeks, trees, gullies, and roads they found. In 1816 the surveyor William Rector and others moved section-by-section west from St. Charles County and the Fifth Principal Meridian. Their route west lay in a broad prairie separating the waters of the Missouri and Mississippi Rivers. Virtually no streams had to be crossed, so travelers could choose any route they wished.

Still, Rector noted "Boons Lick road" only when he neared the Loutre River. There was only one good ford of the Loutre and all the smaller, almost random, tracks converged near it. Rector began his work in Township 48 North, Range 4 West, and continued west to T48N R7W. Since he alone surveyed the area, we cannot say that one surveyor noted the BLR and another did not. The specific locations where Rector described the Road crossing a section are marked on the map in the guide section of this book. In addition, the sidebar on GLO Surveys shows one page from the surveyor's notes indicating the BLR.

The Government Land Office Surveys

The survey of the Fifth Principal Meridian was successfully concluded in our area January 31, 1816. This meridian and its base line in Arkansas are the basis for the public land surveys not just for Missouri but also for Iowa, Arkansas, North Dakota, and parts of Minnesota and South Dakota. To complete that task in such a short time was certainly amazing, but now further work had to be completed.

Once the meridian and base line are surveyed, contracts are issued to survey the townships and then, when the townships are concluded, another contract is made for the section lines. The basic unit, the township, is six miles by six miles and then further divided into thirty-six one-mile square sections. If we imagine a grid beginning at the intersection of the principal meridian and the base line, we can see that the first "row" of townships north of the base line is Township 1 North, often written simply T 1 N. Applying this method to the part of Missouri we are interested in, we can locate it at Township 48 North, T 48 N. And, since each township is six miles on a side, we can determine that it lies 288 miles north of the base line in Arkansas (6 miles times 48 townships).

Now we can use the same system to move east and west from the meridian. The example shown in this sidebar is T 48 N, R 6 W. We are thus in the 48th row north of the baseline and 6 rows west of the meridian. St. Charles, on the other hand, lies east of the meridian so the city's description is T 46 N, R 5 E. That is, it is five townships east of the meridian, which is the county line separating Warren and St. Charles Counties.

The surveyor locates an earlier surveyed corner of his assigned township and begins laying out north-south and east-west lines making one-mile square sections. The example given here shows how the sections must be numbered. The team starts in a corner of the section and moves north, noting elements of interest (especially soil quality and forest cover). He uses a "chain" to measure distances along the route. His chain has 100 "links" in addition to chains for distance. There are 80 chains in one mile. If we divide one mile (5280 feet) by eighty chains, we learn that a chain is 66 feet in length. (One of these chains is exhibited at the museum in Arrow Rock State Park).

T 48 N, R 6 W

6	5	4	3	2	1
7	8	9	10	11	12
18	17	16	15	14	13
19	20	21	22	23	24
30	29	28	27	26	25
31	32	33	34	35	36

This shows a township with 36 sections, each one mile on a side. I have marked the points where the surveyor noted the "Boons Lick road."
Van Bibber's tavern was in the center of section 34, as was the Salt Spring.

Township 48 North, Range 6 West is shown with marks indicating the points where the Boone's Lick Road is mentioned in the surveyor notes. We really don't know anything about the route of the Road between those marks, as the surveyor only followed the section lines. Later, maps (called plat maps)

Franklin: Epicenter of Western Expansion

Page from Government Land Office survey field notes in 1816

```
North  Bt Sects 33 & 34 T 48 N R 6 W
Chs
  9.25  Elm 12 in dia
 35.67  Mulberry 14 in dia
 40.00  Set 1/4 Sect post from wh W O 10
        in dia brs S 20 E 17 lks & Sugar
        tree 6 in dia brs N 53 W 30 lks
 51.50  Boons Lick road & small creek 8 lks S E
 65.67  Hackberry 22 in dia
 69.00  Suter creek 100 lks S E
 80.00  Set post cor for Sects 27, 28, 33 & 34
        from wh a Sycamore 72 in dia brs
        N 57 E 11 lks & Buckeye 8 in dia
        brs S 15 W 27 lks
        Land partly Suter bottom 1st rate
        soil & partly hilly 2nd rate soil
        Timber on the hills W O N Ky & in
        bottom Sycamore, Buckeye, Hackbury
        Red Bud Briers &c
        Near the centre of Sect 34 is a Salt
        Spring sufficiently strong for making salt
        Called Suter Lick
```

The surveyor is running a line north from the southeast corner of section 33. He noted the "Boons Lick road" at 51.50 chains.

were drawn using the field notes, but the lines drawn on those maps are just guesses as to where the Road went.

At the top of this page from a surveyor's notebook you will see that it indicates the surveyor went north between (Bt) sections (Sects) 33 and 34, Township 48 North Range 6 West. At 9.25 chains (nine chains and 25 links), or 610 feet, he notes an elm tree that is 12 inches in diameter. At 35.67 chains, he notes a 14-inch mulberry. He placed a post at 40 chains, the halfway point on the section line, so that further divisions of the section into half and quarter sections can be made later.

At 51.50 chains, the surveyor came to our Boons Lick road. This discovery is noted on June 20, 1816. He crosses Luter creek (the Loutre River) at 69 chains and notes that it is 100 links wide and flows southeast (SE). I chose this particular page from the notes because it is so full of information. The surveyor comments on the bottom of the page that there is a Salt spring called Luter Lick that is sufficiently strong to make salt. He puts it in the center of section 34. This of course is near the ford of the Loutre at Mineola.

Boons Lick road is mentioned at 10 places in the notes and each is on the close approach to the ford at the Loutre River. When the surveyor entered the words "Boons Lick road," he may have been the first to use that name.

The ford at the Loutre River was well known by 1816. Nathan Boone held a Spanish land grant that included the ford and nearby salt lick. His older brother Daniel Morgan Boone had a grant adjacent to his. Nathan had led Clark's force over this same ford in 1808. In 1816 there was a well-defined road here and Isaac Van Bibber, Nathan Boone's brother by adoption, would build his famous tavern here too.

The BLR quickly became the preferred way to travel from St. Charles to the Boone's Lick Country. A man could now load his family in a wagon and easily go west to claim his fortune. Of the two principal BLR routes, the first followed more or less the route that Clark and Boone had pioneered in 1808. After crossing the Loutre, it headed northwest and finally almost due west, passing about five miles north of today's Columbia. This route was used exclusively until 1822, when travelers began to travel on the second, somewhat longer, route.

Because the communities of Columbia (founded in 1819 as Smithton) and Fulton (founded in 1825) offered amenities to Road travelers not available on the early route, the Road shifted south through these towns. Near Williamsburg, the new Road went southwest to Fulton, west to Columbia, and finally west to Rocheport, where it rejoined the earlier route at a point north of that town and headed on to Franklin.

Franklin was certainly the capital of the Boone's Lick Country. Laid out in 1816, the town was considered the "gateway to the Boonslick El Dorado," according to Jonas Viles. Howard County, much larger then, was organized the same year. Franklin began with 97 platted lots in 1816 but was later expanded to 678. Its public square included two acres, and the street on the river side of the square was called St. Charles Street.

One can see from the included map (based on the 1820 Federal census) that greater St. Louis (including St. Charles) and Franklin dominate the territory. The Missouri *Intelligencer*, which began publishing in 1819 in Franklin, reported in an early edition that

> During the month of October it is stated that no less than 271 wagons and four-wheeled carriages and 55 two-wheeled carriages and carts passed near St. Charles, bound principally for Boone's Lick. It is calculated that the number of persons accompanying these wagons, etc. could not be less than three thousand (3000).

The St. Louis *Enquirer*, at about the same time, wrote that twenty wagons per week passed through St. Charles for the past ten weeks and perhaps 12,000 settlers had moved to Howard County. These figures likely cannot be entirely correct but at any rate, many people were moving west through St. Charles for Howard County in 1819.

The establishment of the land office in Franklin in November 1818 had apparently opened the floodgates to torrents of migrants. Many newcomers came from Kentucky and traveled back and forth to that state. Viles claimed that this section of the Boone's Lick (around Franklin) did not go through a frontier stage. He wrote about the new settlers, that "many of them were persons of some means who brought slaves, blooded stock, and considerable cash with them."

Missouri Population Density 1820

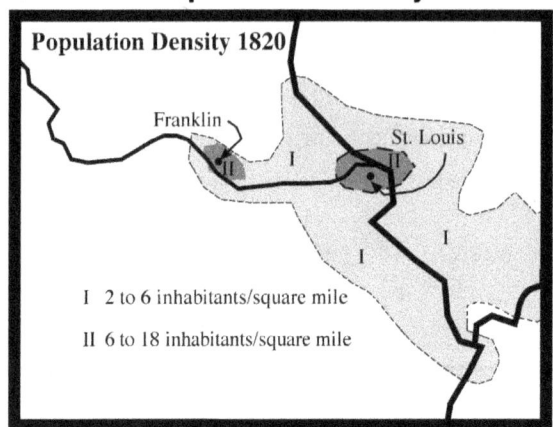

Missouri population density based on the 1820 federal census. It is somewhat congruent with Charles Paullin's map in Atlas of the Historical Geography of the United States.

Once the land office opened for business in Franklin, sales were dramatic. From the opening in late 1818 until July 1, 1820, a total of 1,168,742 acres were sold for a value of $3, 287,816. Sales in St. Louis, where the other Missouri land office was located, amounted to 811,539 acres, which equaled about two-thirds of the sales in Franklin. The Boone's Lick Country was a true phenomenon on the outer frontier.

Population distribution and numbers mirrored the land sales. Howard County had the largest population with 13,426, which included 2,089 slaves. Population in Missouri was found primarily in the Missouri River valley corridor in 1820. The river, after all, was the principal highway at the time. Six counties along the river accounted for well over half of the soon-to-be state's citizens. My estimate would place the population of the Boone's Lick Country at 20,385, which was over thirty percent of the total for Missouri. The percentage of slaves by county did not deviate much from the state's fifteen percent, as it was sixteen in Howard County.

The steamboat Independence arrived in Franklin in 1819, bringing great optimism to the residents, who assumed that regular service would ensue. The next steamboat did not arrive until 1826, however, at a time when Franklin was fading because of Missouri River high waters. By 1819, stagecoaches were making weekly trips from St. Louis to Franklin, but most people still came west by keelboat or the Boone's Lick Road.

The Boone's Lick Road continued in importance after statehood in

1821. The Santa Fe Trail (SFT) opened in that year too, and much of the merchandise destined for New Mexico went west on the BLR to Franklin, where the SFT began. Steamboats did not dominate travel and trade westward until the late 1830s. In the early 1840s, travel increased on the BLR because of the thousands of migrants heading west to Oregon country. Later, in 1849, another bump occurred when gold was discovered in California.

Travel on the BLR became of more local importance when the railroads came to dominate trade and commerce after 1859. The railroads and steamboat travel on the Missouri diminished the importance of the BLR. If one desired to go west by wagon or horse, the BLR was still the route used, but many preferred the speed and convenience of the railroads.

I think one has to have been raised on a farm to comprehend the inconveniences brought about by the congruence of a wheeled vehicle and mud. The Boone's Lick Road offered a major challenge for wagons, carriages, and coaches. By mid-century, dozens of plank roads were proposed to address this mud problem, and, in 1851, a plank road was built connecting St. Charles with Cottleville. The planks soon warped and rotted, and by 1864 this road was no longer in use.

MUD

I can't be certain where on the National Old Trails Road this photo was taken but the scene clearly shows the enemy: mud.

A new invention of the late nineteenth century would change forever travel in the United States. The automobile began as a novelty, but by 1900 its potential and utility were recognized. This was especially true after 1908, when Henry Ford introduced the relatively inexpensive Model T, which brought auto ownership to the masses.

Chapter Three

With increasing automobile ownership, organizations demanding better roads proliferated across the country and citizens in Missouri spearheaded this movement. The usual argument over which route should be utilized across Missouri was settled by selection of the central road, chosen in no small part because the Daughters of the American Revolution (DAR) wanted this newly designated route to follow the old and historic roads already here. The Boone's Lick Road and Santa Fe Trail were to become part of the new transcontinental road called the National Old Trails Road, or Ocean-to-Ocean Highway. The DAR marked the Missouri portion of the new road with granite markers in 1913.

Thus, this new National Old Trails Road, sitting on the older BLR, became the cross-state highway for Missouri until the late 1920s. In the mid-1920s, the national highway numbering system was adopted, and the Missouri cross-state highway became US Rte. 40. Route 40 does not follow the older roads in its entire course. In the guide portion of this book, the important differences will be noted.

National Old Trails Road

The National Old Trails Road in about 1920. It followed the BLR in most locations but notice that by this time it separates from the BLR west of Dardenne and goes through Wentzville and Foristell.

Chapter Four
St. Charles County

St. Charles City

The best location to begin a tour of the route of the Boone's Lick Road is in St. Charles. It was in this delightful town where most travelers and goods began their westward trip whether by water or by wagon. The corridor along the Missouri was the region's fastest-growing during the early historic period, and St. Charles' position on the river and close to St. Louis made it a natural hub.

Today the city has a neat grid-pattern of streets, as do most American towns. The initial street (now Main Street) was established parallel to the river and just above the waters' edge. As time passed, Second Street was created parallel to, and behind, Main Street. Third Street was platted and in place by about 1800. On the other hand, Henry Vest Bingham, writing in his diary in 1818, claimed St. Charles had but "one street which takes up all the space between the shore and the bluffs. It extends along the shore about a mile."

42   Chapter Four

James Campbell said almost the exact thing in 1819 when he wrote, "it has but one street and the bluffs are so close to the river here that there is not room for more."

Running back from Main Street were paths leading from the river; these paths became streets too, which completed today's pattern. The only route not part of this grid was Boone's Lick Road, which angled southwest from Main Street toward the city's common fields. It paralleled Blanchette Creek, more or less, to the top of the hill. Population in 1800 was about 900. In 1850 the city had almost 1599 residents, and by 1900 the total was about 8,000.

A happy event for the city was its selection to be the state's temporary capital in 1821. A site for the permanent capital had been chosen along the Missouri River about halfway across the state. However, while Jefferson City was being built the authorities chose St. Charles to be the temporary capital over eight other cities. Thus, from 1821 until 1826 the state government met over a hardware store on Main Street in St. Charles.

The following sites will help in understanding the value of St. Charles' contributions. Their location can be found on the accompanying map.

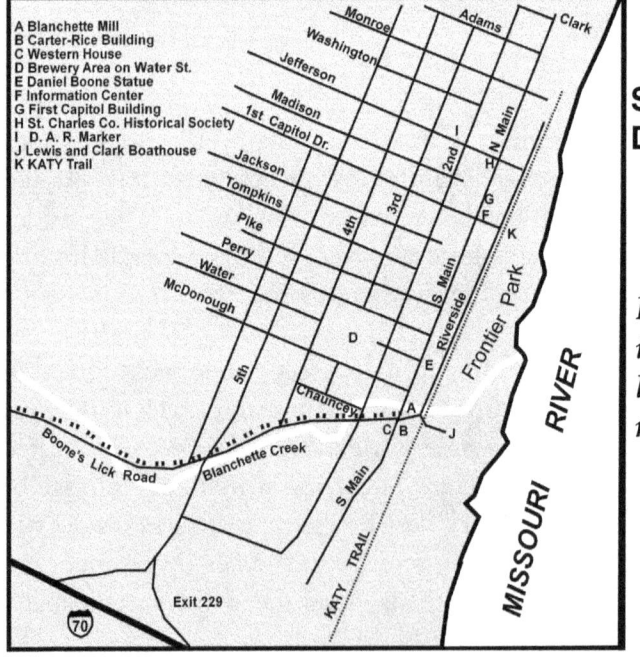

St. Charles Historic District

Locations mentioned in the text can be located from this map.

A. Blanchette Mill

Located on the northeast corner of South Main and Boone's Lick Road, this mill was likely constructed in the late 18th century by Louis Blanchette, the city's founder. Power for the mill was provided by Blanchette Creek, which crossed under South Main here and then continued to the Missouri on the north side of the mill. Louis Blanchette supposedly built the mill in the "French" manner with vertical log walls. Afterwards, it was converted to a more conventional building, with many later additions. Part of the 1790 building (not the log portion, which has not survived) is still visible inside. At the time of writing, the building is a brewpub but it has seen many lives: woolen mill, prison, hospital, corncob pipe factory (1900), and, in 1917, it was listed on the Sanborn fire insurance map as a Negro tenement.

Blanchette Creek

This creek supplied the water for the Blanchette Mill and perhaps one other.

B. Carter-Rice Building

The Carter-Rice building is located on the southeast corner of the Boone's Lick Road/South Main intersection. It was built in about 1840 as the Boone's Lick Trail Inn. Over the years, it has also been used as a cold-water flat for multiple families. For the last thirty years, it has served as a bed and breakfast inn.

Western House and the Boone's Lick Road

The eastern terminus of the BLR at South Main and Blanchette Creek.

C. Western House

This building began as a hotel and saloon serving the thirsty and tired travelers utilizing the Boone's Lick Road. Behind the hotel were stables and a blacksmith shop to tend to the travelers' stock. The Western House went through many lives as tenement and boarding house before becoming what it is today, an art gallery.

Now, walk north on South Main Street.

D. Brewery area on Water Street

Water Street is named for the five springs that were located just one and a half blocks west of Main Street. The water from the springs formed a small creek here in earlier times. Beginning about 1850 a brewery could be found about where Third Street would intersect Water Street (Water ends now at Second Street). The last of these breweries closed in the 1970s.

E. Daniel Boone Statue

A very nice statue of Daniel Boone is located in a small space on the river side of South Main. The Boone's Lick in Howard County was named for Daniel's two sons, Nathan and Daniel Morgan, who managed the salt works in the early part of the nineteenth century. The area around the Lick became known as Boone's Lick Country. It was to this larger "country" that the Road headed.

Daniel Boone   **Trail to Fort Osage**

Daniel Boone came to live in Missouri in 1799, bringing many American families with him. He and the others made their homes in the Boone Settlement near Femme Osage Creek. A side trip to the very important settlement is included in this book.

There is also a new historical marker at this site, which correctly describes the opening of a trail from St. Charles to Jackson County, Missouri, in 1808. This trail was the result of the need for a fort and trading post (Fort Osage) in the western part of Missouri. Nathan Boone guided William Clark from St. Charles westward, taking a route which in most cases was followed by the later Boone's Lick Road in 1816.

F. Information Center

The Center stands at the northeast corner of Jefferson and South Main. Parking is directly behind the building. It is a place filled with helpful people and useful information. Walking-tour pamphlets are available here as well as audio directions for a comprehensive tour of the old city. Next to the parking lot is a replica of a "dog trot" log house. This style of house was very commonly built along the Boone's Lick Road in the early nineteenth century. You will see several of these as you take the tour. Most are now covered with wooden siding.

G. First Capitol Building

This Federal-style brick building served as the temporary capitol for the new state of Missouri from 1821 until 1826. Charles and Ruloff Peck owned the building and continued their business on the street level while the second floor was divided into Senate and House chambers. It is open to the public for a modest entrance fee.

H. St. Charles County Historical Society

The Society is housed in the Market and Fish building on the southwest corner of Jefferson and South Main. The building was constructed beginning in the 1820s. The Society has an extensive collection of photos and documents related to the history of the county. It houses archives, publications, and family history areas, and the staff provides much helpful information for the public. They also sell some books of value to Road scholars.

I. Daughters of the American Revolution Marker

Dozens of markers have been placed along the Boone's Lick Road by the Daughters of the American Revolution (hereinafter DAR). The one here in St. Charles should be considered the first in the series for the Boone's Lick Road. Find the Courthouse Square, which fills a block between Jefferson, 2nd, Washington, and 3rd, and locate the DAR marker on the southeast corner. DAR markers were placed along the Road beginning in 1913 and run all the way to the Boone's Lick in Howard County. From Howard County, additional markers denote the Santa Fe Trail as far as Santa Fe, New Mexico. It really was quite an achievement to place these markers, and the work was accomplished at a time that people living along the routes remembered when these were actually primitive roads. For that matter, in 1913 the roads were still very primitive, as you will see later in this guide.

J. Lewis and Clark Boat House

St. Charles is taken with the Lewis and Clark mystique. Their expedition really began here in 1804 and they remained here for some time planning their

First Capitol Building

Photo was taken early in the morning to avoid the many cars usually parked in front of the building. Note the steps leading down fom the right side of the photo. Main Street is slightly higher than the KATY trail behind it.

Dog Trot House

This is a replica of the common dog trot house style. Two rooms are separated by a breezeway. This type of building was a common one for early taverns along the BLR.

trip. The Boat House holds replicas of the keelboat and pirogues used by the expedition, and since travel west from St. Charles before 1816 was on the river it is important to see what these common boats looked like. The Museum is at 1050 S. Riverside Drive, and not far from the Blanchette Mill.

K. KATY Trail

You have crossed the KATY Trail by now and may wonder what it is. The Missouri-Kansas-Texas Railroad ran from St. Charles to Texas until late in the last century. Its rail bed is now the KATY Trail, a hiking and biking trail that runs from St. Charles to Clinton, Missouri. It closely follows the north bank of the Missouri River, finally crossing the river at Boonville. At a spot just before it crosses the river, the railroad passed through Franklin, which was the short-lived "capital" of Boone's Lick Country.

ST. CHARLES TO THE WEST

Leave St. Charles by taking Boone's Lick Road, which will be paralleling Blanchette Creek. As you climb the hill, you will see a brick house at 22 Route B (it is on your left, about three-quarters of a mile from South Main). This is Old Man Schaffer's Tavern; it was constructed about 1833 and served as a tavern until about 1870.

Continue past South 5th (stop light here), climbing gently until you reach the intersection of Route 94 and Interstate 70. Kate Gregg, writing in 1933, said, "from Main Street in St. Charles, up Blanchette Creek and to the top of the hill, it [the Boone's Lick Road] is more or less unimproved, and reminiscent of bygone days."

It is a bit tricky at the above intersection, but you should follow the signs for "South on 94." Then follow 94 for 6.1 miles (at the time of writing, this highway is under construction and not a joy to drive). Gregg, in the same 1933 article, wrote, "From the top of the hill almost to the marker set up by the DAR to indicate the site of Nicholas Coontz's Fort, the modern road scrapers have been ravaging high, wide, and deep." Times have not changed much here.

One detour you might want to take along Hwy. 94 is to view a Latter Day Saints Boone's Lick Road Marker just a few blocks off Hwy. 94. To get there, look for the exit to Pralle Ln. at 1.5 miles from the Interstate, where you turn right and then, in one block, turn left onto Old Hwy. 94. Drive on 94 to 2245 S. Old Hwy. 94, where you will find the marker in front of the LDS church. When you finish you can either retrace your steps to get back to 94 or continue on Old 94, which eventually rejoins modern 94.

The Mormons began their migration to Missouri in 1831, and most of the time used the BLR to get to Jackson County (Independence, near Kansas City). The Missouri *Intelligencer* in 1833 told of more than one hundred Mormons in Howard County waiting to move on to Independence. The writer of the article went on to say that "there were about 4 to five hundred Mormons collected at Zion (Independence)." In 1838 and 1839, about 10,000 Mormons were driven out of Missouri, ending up temporarily in Illinois. The Mormons certainly used the BLR to go west from St. Charles, and it is likely they used the early version of the BLR in order to avoid Fulton and Columbia.

St. Charles to Cottlesville

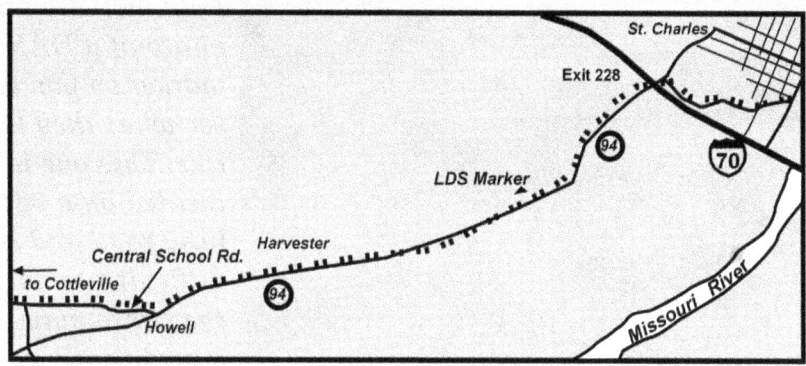

A short guide to the Boone Settlement can be found immediately following this chapter. There are three easy ways to drive to the Settlement from the BLR. The first way is to continue on Highway 94 instead of turning at Central School Road. Highway 94 goes to the town of Defiance, which will lead you to the Settlement. The second opportunity will come at the intersection of State Route N (the BLR) and Highway Z. Turning left there will take you to New Melle and on to the Boone Home. The third way is at the county line where you should turn left on Hwy. T, which will lead you to Marthasville at the western end of the Settlement.

The old Boone's Lick Road is mostly to your right here and on a local map is designated S. Old Highway 94. Look for a cross street with a signal light called Central School Road, where you should turn right. This road will have several names so do not be alarmed. Signs may say "County Road N" or "Boone's Lick Road." You will be driving on top of the old Road for the next few miles. Continue on this road to Mid-River Mall Drive, where there is a stoplight. Then continue straight and look immediately to your right (north side) for a DAR marker in the middle of a lot labeled Kountz' Fort 1800. The fort was about one-quarter mile behind the marker, near a natural pond (still there). Rangers built the fort during the War of 1812 to protect settlers from Indian attacks. After the war ended, Nicholas Kountz maintained a tavern here.

DAR Marker at Kountz Fort

I am including this photo of a DAR marker so you can see what they look like. This one is located on a very busy road and is difficult to visit so the photo may have to suffice.

Kountz had constructed two mills on his property by 1803. When Henry Vest Bingham visited Kountz in 1818 he noted that the mill was badly constructed and was handicapped by the dry weather. He went on to write, "But for Nine months it might Do a Great Buissness as there is Suficient water to Drive two pair of Stones if it was well Constructed around this Mill is Some Good Timber..." John M. Peck, who went by the tavern that same year, said of Nicholas Kountz that he was "a rough, wicked, and yet hospitable old German."

COTTLEVILLE

Continue west on this road (now called Hwy. N) until it dead-ends at a church parking lot, where you turn right, following Route N. You are now in the village of Cottleville, an important location on the early BLR. Records show that by 1800 there was a settlement at Cottleville and that mills were built on the creek here by 1803 if not before. Gregg found sources claiming that the road from St. Charles to the Dardenne was designated the Highway to Dardenne by 1805. This "highway" continued west to what was later Pond Fort.

Cottleville

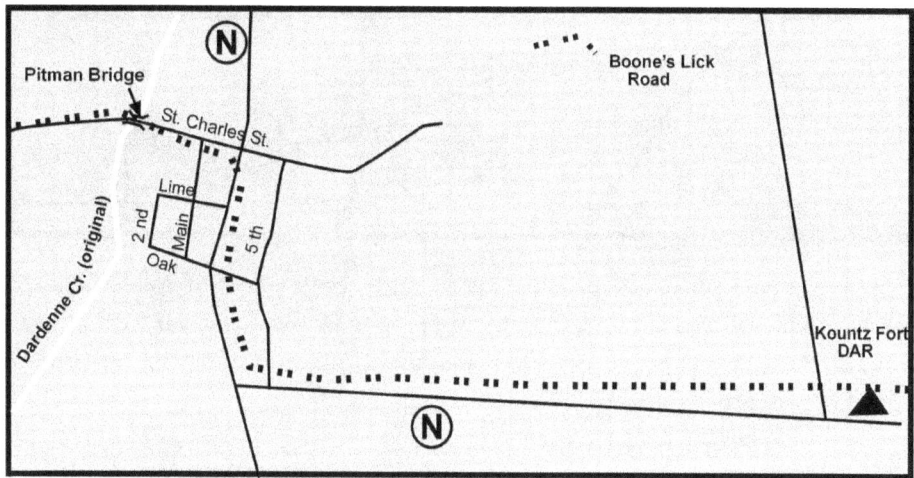

Here in Cottleville the road west forded Dardenne Creek, the only significant stream that the BLR crossed until it encountered the Loutre River in Montgomery County. Cottleville was named for the Cottle family, who held a Spanish land grant here in 1798. Warren Cottle had the grant that encompasses the town. A short-lived plank road called the Western Plank Road ran from Cottleville to St. Charles in the 1850s but lasted only until the 1860s.

Drive on N north a few blocks to St. Charles Street and turn left. Even the name, St. Charles, tells us that this was the road to St. Charles. You are on the BLR as you drive the block downhill to the Pitman Bridge, named for John Pitman, a prominent local landowner in the early nineteenth century. The bridge is a dandy. Park your car and get out to look at the underside of the bridge, noting the fine stonework. The bridge spans the old course of Dardenne Creek, which was rerouted some decades ago. The BLR went straight west here on the dirt road that you see. Turn around here, retrace your steps to Route N, and turn left to follow it. The highway makes a big swing north and then goes west, finally coming close to the "new" Dardenne Creek. The road makes a turn to the right, at which point you are back on the BLR.

After turning northwest on Rte. N, and driving about one mile, you will see on the left the beautiful stone house of Capt. James Campbell. Campbell, who had served in the War of 1812, constructed the house in 1836. Later, the building served as an inn.

Cottleville to Pond Fort

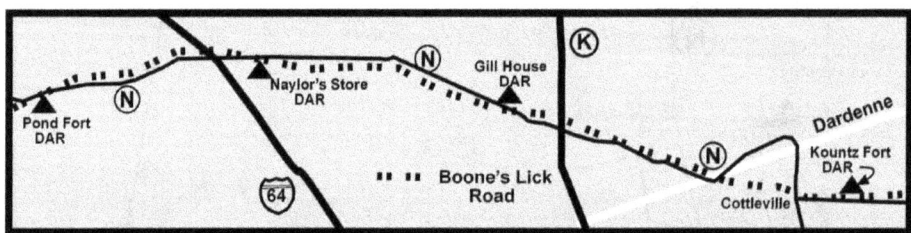

Remain on Rte. N, passing Rte. K and, about one-half mile farther, on the left, you will see the Gill House Millstones in the front yard of a house. The three millstones serve as a DAR marker commemorating the mill built by John Gill near this spot in 1821.

Pitman Bridge

Soulard Grant Map of Warren Cottle

Warren Cottle was one of the first settlers in this area. If you look closely in the lower right-hand corner of the map you will see "Riv Dardenne." This is about where Cottleville is located today. Courtesy of the Missouri State Archives.

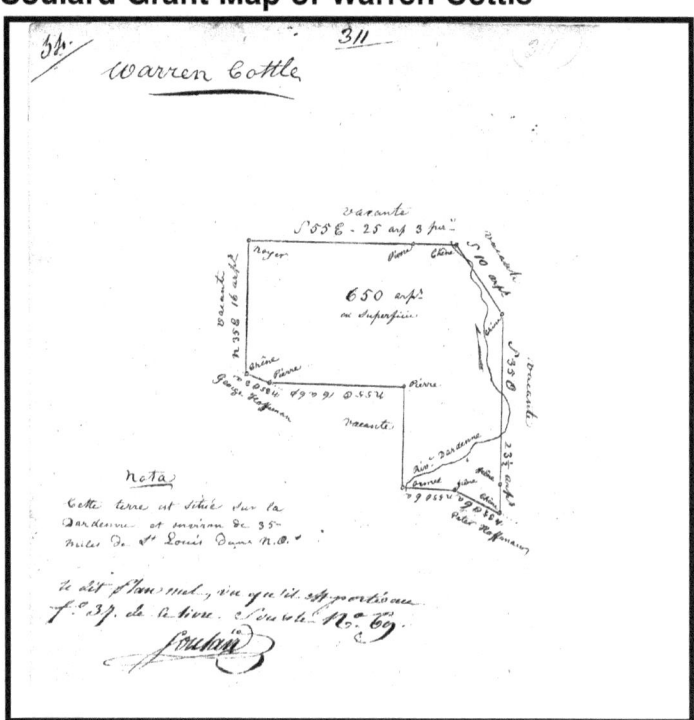

Pitman Bridge

The underside of the bridge reveals the nice stone construction.

You are traversing the Dardenne Prairie now, and you will note from the included maps how the BLR threaded its way, keeping to the high ground between Dardenne Creek to the south and Peruque Creek to the north. BLR travelers used this same strategy until they reached the Loutre River.

About three miles west of the Gill House DAR you will see a DAR marker for the site of John Naylor's store. Naylor was one of the founders of the town of Dardenne. The marker is on the north side of N in front of a house.

POND FORT

Past the Naylor store marker is Interstate 64 but you must stay on Rte. N. To accomplish this, drive over the Interstate, where Rte. N changes names to Hawk Ridge Road for a short span. You will come to a stoplight where you must turn left to join N again. After rejoining N, in about three miles you will come to the site of Pond Fort. Built by Rangers during the War of 1812 and housing only one family, the fort had space for the other families who lived nearby in time of danger. William Clark wrote of the pond here (the fort was, of course, not here at that time) as he traveled west in 1808: "Encamped at a Pond at the out Skirts of the Settlement in a butifull Plain, near a few low trees." The fort was built later on the south side of Rte N, close to the DAR marker "Pond Fort."

Pond Fort

Pond Fort in about 1900. Photo courtesy Missouri State Historical Society.

St. Charles County 55

According to Captain John R. Bell, the official journalist for the Stephen Long expedition, he and Long visited the Fort in 1820. Bell wrote that the fort was "constructed of logs and a square, whose sides are about 200 feet, having block houses at each of the angles, in the interior, and joining to the sides are erected cabins for accommodations of families, when they resort to the fort for safety." He went on to commend Mr. Baily, who resided here and kept "excellent entertainment for travelers." Bell also noted that three notches on the trees marked the way through the woods here. Hence, it was called the "Three notched road."

Continue on Rte. N to the west. The road curves many times in this area as it skirts the headwaters of various creeks. You will pass Timberland High School on your right. Note the DAR marker next to the road in front of the school. The marker was moved here from its original location farther along. Those using Dan Rothwell's book *Along the Boone's Lick Road* will note the change of location that occurred after the book was published. The marker notes the Boone Settlement, which is south of here.

Pond Fort to Kenner's Tavern

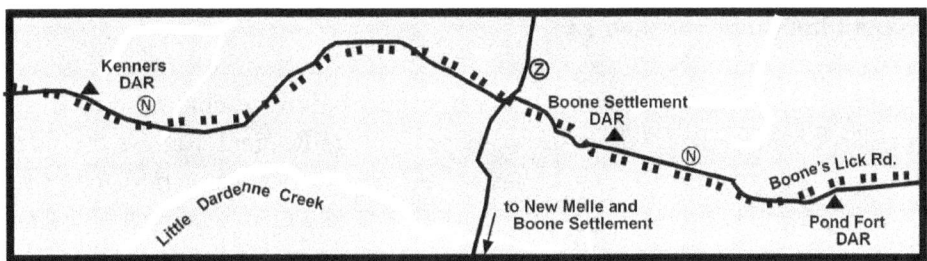

You are approaching the intersection of state routes N and Z, where the above-mentioned DAR marker was originally placed, and labeled "Boone's Home" and a few other items related to Boone's Settlement. If you wish to visit the Settlement, you can turn left here onto Rte. Z and descend through New Melle, a German immigrant community from the 1830s, and on to Nathan Boone's home and other Settlement sites. Those are all covered in a side trip in this book and turning here gives you a picturesque entrance to the Settlement.

On the other hand, if you want to continue following the BLR, go straight through the intersection and remain on Rte. N. This piece of St.

Charles County was thinly populated until after the Indian threat during the War of 1812 subsided in 1815 or 1816. Look for a barn on your right about five miles west of the intersection. In the bushes across the road to the left is a DAR marker "Kenners Tavern 1819." The date is far too early, as Rodman Kenner did not arrive in Missouri until 1834. Nevertheless, whenever the tavern was built, Kenner ran it until his death in 1876. It was a popular stop on the BLR.

A note here on the word "tavern." In the early nineteenth century, a tavern was what we call an inn, a place for travelers to stay over. They likely served hard cider with their meals, but that was the drink of choice since it was safe.

Your author will make a guess about this tavern and its earlier owner. Colonel John Glover traveled west along the BLR in 1826 and back again later in the year. On his way west he "traveled on and tarried all night McConnols, bill 62 1/2 cents." On his way east he wrote, "Came on to Mr. McConnols for breakfast the best house I stoped at in the State of Missouri bill 37 1/2 cents." Glover had stayed the night before at Mr. Pringles at Hickory Grove (you will visit that site a bit farther along) and the trip to breakfast would certainly have brought him to the Kenner site.

Follow Rte. N to a stop sign at Rte. T. You may have noticed an old building half-covered in trees to your right just before reaching the intersection. This is Meridian Hall, so-called because State Route T follows the Fifth Principal Meridian here. The hall has served many functions: school, community center, and church. This very important line, the Fifth Principal Meridian, was the first surveyed in Missouri in 1815 by the US government. The Government Land Office survey crew began their work at the point where the Arkansas entered the Mississippi (in the state of Arkansas now). It took the crew many months to reach this point, but no other surveys could be done until this meridian was marked.

The Boone's Lick Road left St. Charles County here and entered Warren County. You will need to drive straight across Rte. T into Warren County to continue the tour.

You could also turn left here, drive to the Missouri River to Marthasville, and visit the Boone Settlement.

SIDE TRIP TO BOONE SETTLEMENT

"The warp of nature and the weft of human activity create a tapestry of varied and wonderful cultural landscapes." - H.J.

One of Missouri's most interesting and attractive cultural landscapes is located southwest of St. Charles. Called the Boone Settlement, this area is named for Col. Daniel Boone and his many followers who settled here in the twilight of the eighteenth century. These were the folks who cut the trees, built houses and mills, and chose the routes for trails and roads.

The Spanish authorities wanted Spaniards to settle in Upper Louisiana following Spain's acquisition in 1763. But by the 1790s, the authorities knew these plans had failed and they were content with the many French that came from Canada. The same authorities also attempted to bolster their defenses against British intrusions, especially to the north between the upper Missouri and the Great Lakes. Finally, reluctantly, they turned to the Americans. The Americans were not Catholic, a drawback, but they were fiercely anti-British so they were invited to cross the river into Spanish territory. The newcomers were allowed to obtain land grants in Missouri and, by settling here, they would bolster the frontier against the British and the occasional Indian intrusions from the west, or so the Spanish thought.

What started as a trickle of Americans in the 1790s became a flood in 1799 and thereafter. One area in particular that attracted American settlers was near the Missouri River about where Femme Osage Creek enters the river. Daniel Morgan Boone, one of Col. Boone's sons who had received a grant of land in 1797, brought a few slaves with him and put them to work clearing the land and planting a crop. His grant, which lay southwest of St. Charles and near the Missouri River on its left, or north, bank, would form the nucleus of the Boone Settlement.

Boone Settlement

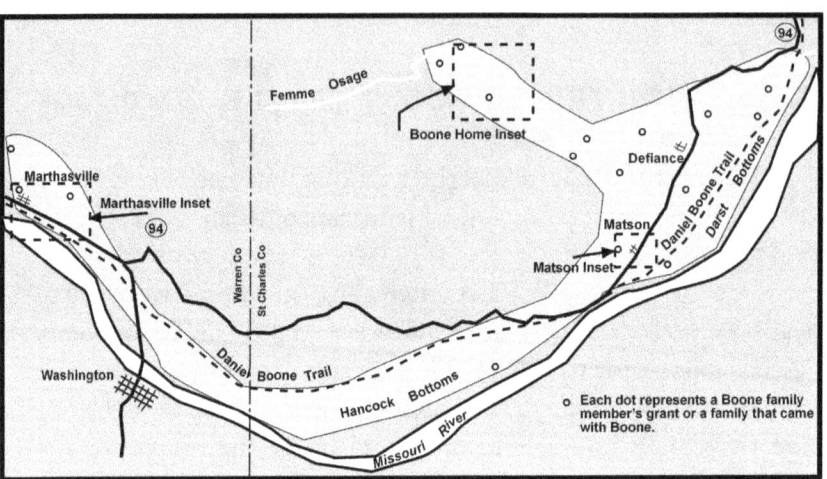

Daniel Morgan returned to Kentucky to visit his father with a letter from the Spanish Lt. Governor inviting Daniel Boone to come to Upper Louisiana (later Missouri) to establish a colony of Americans. The Colonel had suffered many financial misfortunes in Kentucky so he was primed for a move that offered a fresh start. In late 1799 and 1800 Col. Boone, along with the Callaways, Bryans, Hayses, Buchanans, Clays, Van Bibbers, and the Halls, began their trek west. Some went by pirogue (small boat) while others went overland, driving their livestock before them.

On arrival in Missouri, Boone claimed land adjacent to his son D. M. Boone's grant along the Missouri River, just upstream from its confluence with Femme Osage Creek. Boone was allowed to secure grants for all who accompanied him from Kentucky. The included map shows this tight assemblage of Boone's extended family. Later, some of the clan moved upriver 20 miles to incorporate the older French village of La Charrette. For example, Flanders Callaway, one of the Colonel's sons-in-law, moved to La Charrette (near today's Marthasville) and the Colonel lived with the Callaways following the death of his wife Rebecca in 1813 until his own death in 1820. He and his wife Rebecca were buried in a small cemetery near Marthasville. Col. Boone was appointed comandante of the Femme Osage district, one of seven such districts in Missouri during the Spanish

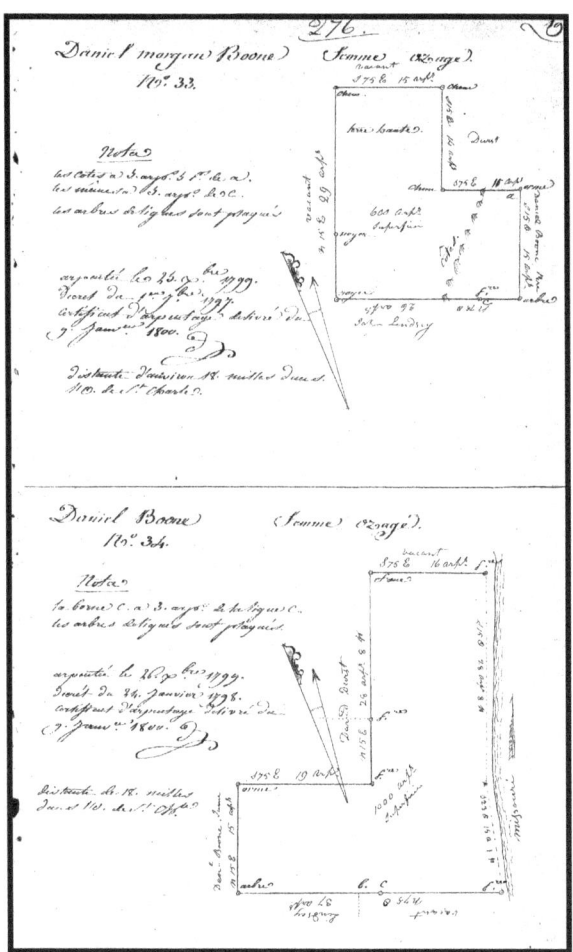

This Soulard map combining maps of Daniel Morgan Boone's (top) and Col. Daniel Boone's (bottom) grants. Note on D.M. Boone's grant the wavey line cutting across the southeast corner. That line represents the dividing line between the "bottoms" (East) and the uplands to the left.
Courtesy of the Missouri State Archives.

control. A comandante was the civil and military leader and the judge of civil cases within his district. James MacKay, an Irishman turned Spaniard, was comandante of another mostly American district, San Andres, across the river from the Boone Settlement.

The Americans that Boone commanded never were called upon by the Spanish to defend the territory but, ironically, these Americans played a very important role during the War of 1812. Nathan Boone and his brother Daniel Morgan both commanded U. S. Ranger companies during the war; these companies were filled with Callaways, Hayses, and Van Bibbers. The rangers constructed forts for defense as well as making forays against Indian threats. The British were not directly involved, but their surrogates the Fox and Sauk Indians posed a constant threat against Missouri settlers until late in 1815, almost a year after the War officially ended.

Two defensive forts were built during the war in the Boone Settlement. One was at Daniel Morgan Boone's home, near present-day Matson. Another was located at the Flanders Callaway house, near today's Marthasville. "Forting up," as it was called, generally meant fortifying an existing house by building a palisade around it. Cattle and other livestock would be kept within the palisade walls to protect them from Indian raiders.

> Author's Note: I have to keep reminding myself that this book is about the Boone's Lick Road. It is so easy and rewarding to dwell on Col. Daniel Boone, but Boone was not really a large part of the BLR story. His sons and family comprise an important element in its history, however, and visiting the Boone Settlement helps round out their story. Nathan and Daniel Morgan Boone both were important in the defense of Missouri during the War of 1812. Together they blazed a trail called the Boone Trace to the Boone's Lick in Howard County, where in about 1805 they started boiling salty water from springs for making salt for the settlements. Several years later Nathan guided William Clark from St. Charles to near present-day Kansas City, where they built Fort Osage; the route Nathan chose, for the most part, became the route of the Boone's Lick Road.

Daniel Boone's Judgment Tree near Matson. This tree has long since disappeared. Photo courtesy of Missouri State Historical Society.

VISITING THE SETTLEMENT TODAY

Visitors can enter the Boone Settlement by a variety of routes and, thus, this section will be mainly an inventory of sites one could visit: (See earlier map "Boone Settlement" for location of inset maps.)

Sites near the Boone Home
(A) The Nathan Boone home was constructed of stone. Tax records indicate the house was most likely completed in 1818. Some accounts claim that Daniel Boone helped in the construction, but that is unlikely. Boone did die here in 1820. The house and grounds are owned by Lindenwood University (its main campus is in St. Charles) and are open to the public for a fee. The Flanders Callaway log house was moved here from Marthasville. It was in that house that Daniel Boone's wife Rebecca died and where Boone lived about half his remaining years, according to Boone scholar Ken Kamper.
(B) Upstream (left as one exits the Boone Home parking lot) at about six-tenths of a mile on the left stands the stone house of James Van Bibber, the brother-in-law of Nathan Boone.
(C) Continuing northwest on State Route F, you come to a large stone building that was the Jonathan Bryan oxen-driven mill. The address is 2275

and the sign says "Stone Mill Meadow Farm." Jonathan Bryan was a first cousin of Daniel Boone's wife Rebecca.

Nathan Boone Home

An early photo of the Nathan Boone home in the Femme Osage valley. Although Col. Daniel Boone died here, it was not his home. There are now several historic buildings on the grounds here making the site worth a visit. Photo courtesy Missouri State Historical Society.

Sites near the village of Matson

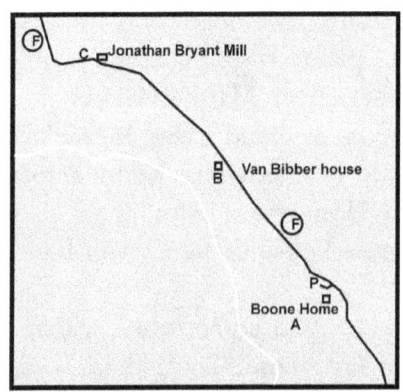
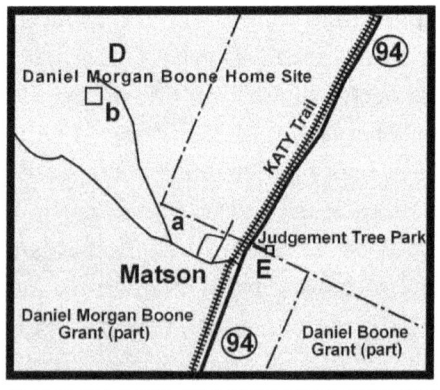

Two very important sites are found near the town of Matson.
(D) First, the log house of Daniel Morgan Boone still exists either on a hill just west of the town ("a" on map) or in the valley several hundred yards to the west ("b" on map), where traditional accounts locate it. This log house is where Daniel and Rebecca Boone lived their first four years in Missouri. It was "forted up" during the War of 1812.

(E) Second, the little park just off Highway 94 on the river side in Matson is called Judgment Tree Park. Parking is available here. There is a nice map showing the extent of the Boone Settlement and a marker with the Daniel Boone story. The famous Judgment Tree stood a couple hundred yards toward the river from the latter marker on the Daniel Boone grant. A few yards south of the parking lot there is a DAR granite trail marker that tells of the original horse trail connecting the Boone Settlement with the salt works near Franklin.

Sites near Marthasville

(F) From the Judgment Tree Park it is an easy and attractive drive west along Highway 94 toward Marthasville, with vineyards and wineries on view. At the junction of Highway 94 and Highway 47, turn right and drive on 47 for nearly 2 miles to Highway D on the right, which leads into Marthasville.

You will also see the KATY Trail along this route. The old MKT Railroad

MARTHASVILLE

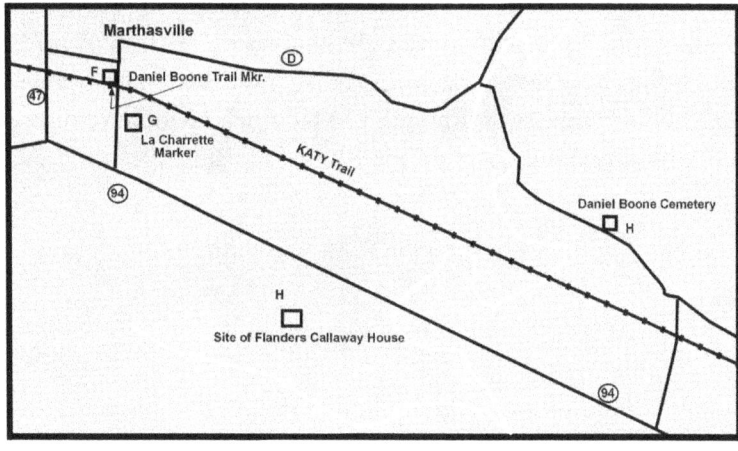

(Missouri, Kansas, and Texas) bed is now a Missouri State Park hiking and biking trail, which is bringing thousands of mostly urbanites to visit the area. It is best to start your visit to Marthasville in the town and adjacent to the Katy Trail Park. This small park has a Daniel Boone Trail marker placed here by the DAR.

(G) Across the KATY Trail toward the river one hundred yards is another pullout for Wessel Park, where you will see a Marthasville marker. Then, near the little house, another marker commemorating the very early westward-most settlement along the Missouri River, "La Charrette," a small French village located one mile to the southwest. Lewis and Clark visited La Charrette in 1804 and, more importantly, Zebulon Pike remained here several days in 1806. Pike received information from residents here that allowed him to make his famous "Map to Santa Fe." The little house was built as part of the Lewis and Clark expedition bicentennial and is in the vertical log tradition of the French.

(H) Return to Highways 94/47, turn left and drive to the sign saying Boone Monument and Burial Site, where you will turn left to the Boone burial site. This is actually called the Bryan Cemetery or Daniel Boone Burial Place. As you left Marthasville, you passed by some fields on your right where the Flanders Callaway house stood before being moved to the Boone Home near Defiance. The road to the cemetery twists a bit and finally you will see the sign to the right. Parking is on the left. There are two markers here for Daniel Boone. The story is that he and Rebecca were buried here, but in 1845 folks from Kentucky came here and disinterred them for removal to Kentucky. Recent research has found that the caskets and bodies had deteriorated to the extent that although the Kentucky people removed the large skeletal bones, certainly part of the bodies remain here.

Original grave of Daniel Boone. Someone stole the bronze marker that was in the opening. Roger Slusher is shown inspecting another marker.

This nice marker replaces the earlier stolen one and is nearby. Boone's wife, Rebecca, was a Bryan and this cemetery is actually the Bryan Cemetery.

Chapter Five

Warren and Montgomery Counties

WARREN COUNTY

At the intersection of Routes T and N, if you continue straight ahead, you will notice the road description changes to Rte. OO for a short distance. You have passed into Warren County and are traversing Hickory Grove Prairie. You can see a DAR marker on the left side, about one-half mile west of the intersection.

The DAR marker is labeled "Hickory Grove 1823." The small booklet that the DAR published giving the historical background for each of their markers states that Thomas Kennedy owned the land in this area. The authors of the booklet go on to say that Kennedy settled here in 1809 and built Kennedy's Fort for protection from Indians during the War of 1812.

Chapter Five

Warren County

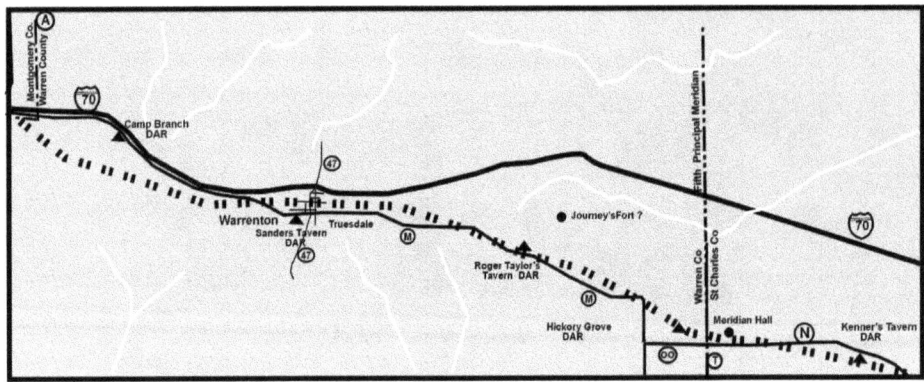

I have some problems with the DAR story above. First, why did the DAR, in 1913 when the marker was set, inscribe 1823? In addition, why didn't the marker mention Kennedy Fort as others had for other forts? The real story, I think, can be found by a careful reading of the journal of John Glover, who passed by twice in 1826. Glover called the owner Mr. Pringle and Glover stayed the night for 37 1/2 cents. The editor of the Glover journal, Marie George Windell, tells us in a footnote that Hickory Grove was settled in 1819 by four families, the Norman Pringle family being one of the four. Norman, she writes, "never hunted but feasted on books."

Beyond the marker, you will come to another intersection, where you should turn right onto Rte. M, which you will follow into Warrenton. These two roads, M and OO, are on section or half-section lines, so they are not on the BLR here. You will resume travel on the BLR a bit after turning west on Rte. M. You are still following the ridge between Peruque and Dardenne Creeks.

Continue on Rte. M and you will see the DAR marker for Roger Taylor's Tavern on the right, north side of the road as you descend a hill. Just north of the Taylor marker lies land that comprised an early land claim of James Journey. John R. Bell wrote that he left Pond Fort at four-thirty in the afternoon and "arrived at Jurnie's some time after dark, a continuous prairie almost the whole distance." There are some sources that claim Journey had a fort here during the War of 1812, but I have my doubts that anyone was living this far west in 1812 when the War started.

WARRENTON

As you approach Warrenton, you may begin to hear the roar of traffic on Interstate 70. Thus far, you have been following the Boone's Lick Road, which, in 1912, became part of the National Old Trails Road. The next iteration of the St. Louis-to-Kansas City highway came in 1927, when US 40 was designated and constructed. This new road did not follow the BLR out of St. Charles. It really was like its successor, Interstate 70. However, here at Warrenton the BLR and US 40 come together and will follow the same basic route in close proximity until we reach Williamsburg.

Continue into Warrenton's Main Street, also named W. Boonslick Rd., and State Hwy. MM. Across from the Courthouse, you can see a DAR marker "Sanders Tavern." Harold Sanders maintained a tavern here at some time, although not as early as 1826, that appears on the marker.

Sanders Tavern DAR Marker

Main Street continues west and where it leaves town it becomes somewhat crooked, which probably indicates it is back on top of the BLR. Eventually, you will reach the south frontage road for the Interstate, which is old US 40.

Stay on the south frontage road, Old US 40, for six miles until you reach another DAR marker for Camp Branch. Early travelers mentioned Camp Branch directly or indirectly. It was a very good campsite on the very eastern edge of Loutre Prairie. James Brown Campbell wrote, "in a few miles we enter a prairie which reaches to the bluffs of Luter Creek." John Glover mentions it by name: "I proceeded on and came to Mr. Prices at Camp Branch in the edge of Luter Prairie where I tarried all night Bill 62 1/2 cents."

After Camp Branch you pass into Montgomery County.

MONTGOMERY COUNTY

When you left the Camp Branch DAR marker, you entered the Loutre Prairie. Campbell described it this way: "We start at dawn of day, the weather clear and warm. In a few miles we enter a prairie which reaches to the bluffs of Luter Creek. 28 miles from our last encampment."

Jonesburg

Old US 40 crosses into Montgomery County just before the small community of Jonesburg. According to Dan Rothwell, the town was not platted until 1858, long after the Cross Keys tavern was built. The tavern was a well-known stop on the BLR after it opened in 1834.

Eastern Montgomery County

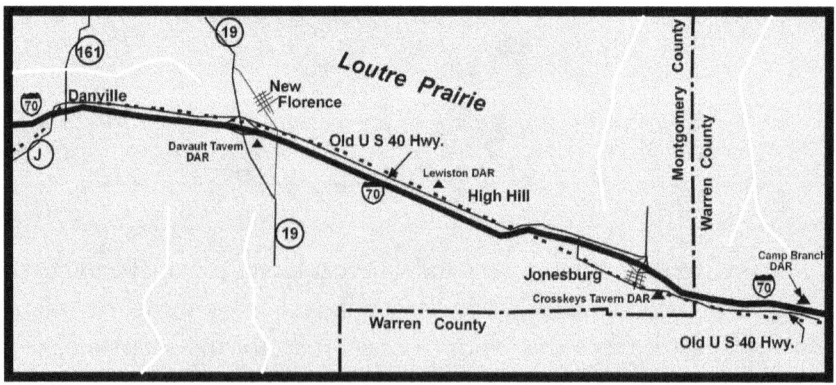

The DAR marker is on the south side of Boone's Lick Road as you enter town. Also of interest is a slave cabin moved here from a farm nearby. Most early settlers came to Missouri from Kentucky and Tennessee and brought a few slaves with them. This cabin is on your left in the center of town.

Jonesburg

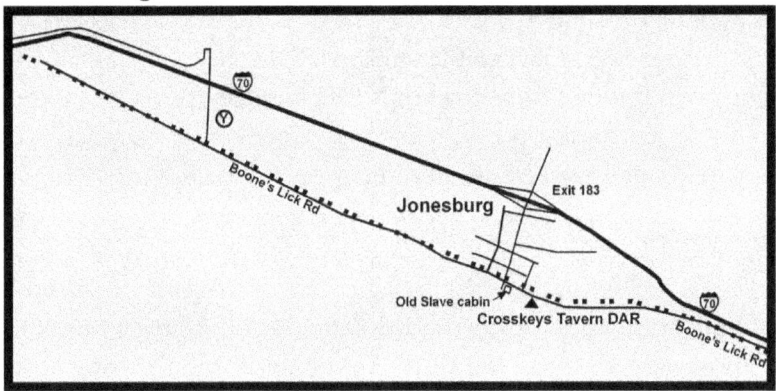

Cross Keys Tavern

Photo of the old Cross Keys tavern. Photo courtesy of the Missouri State Historical Society.

Continue west on the Boone's Lick Road about 1.5 miles to Fleahman Road (Rte. Y), where you should turn north to cross the Interstate, picking up the BLR on the north side of the artery. Next stop is a marker telling you about the short-lived town of Lewiston. Lewiston was first mentioned by Glover in 1826, who said he "past the town of Louiston on the way to Vanbabers." The town was named for Meriwether Lewis and was the county seat of Montgomery County from 1827 to 1833. After the seat was moved to Danville in the latter year, Lewiston languished.

Remain on Boone's Lick Road to New Florence. Across the interstate, on the south side just past a power station, is a marker for Davault Tavern, which was built about 1828 and stood directly on the BLR.

Danville

Continue west on the BLR toward Danville. This small community is one of the most interesting on the BLR. As you approach the town, you will see the Greek Revival Baker Plantation House on the left. The house, built in 1854 by Sylvester Baker, is listed on the National Historic Register. It is important, first because of architectural style. The house is an "I house" in form, with walls 18 inches thick made of brick at the site by slaves owned by Baker. Another reason it is important is that on October 14, 1864, the town of Danville was attacked by troops under the command of William "Bloody Bill" Anderson, who served under Confederate Gen. Sterling Price. Anderson's troops attempted to burn the house but were unsuccessful. Some damage was done to the interior, but the residents managed to put the flames out.

Continue west from the Baker House, where the paved road makes a gentle turn to the left. At this point, the BLR instead went straight ahead through the trees. If you look carefully, you can make out its path. The next house, on your right, is a bit of a mystery. You will view it from its other side in a few minutes. The house is actually built of logs and is a "dog trot" form, two log buildings connected by a central breezeway. (You saw an example of this form of house in St. Charles behind the Visitors Center.) It was probably built as a tavern whose date of construction must have been early, probably in the 1830s.

Log House from south

The view is from the south in this photo. The entry way was moved here to face the new highway, US 40, which opened here about 1928.

Danville

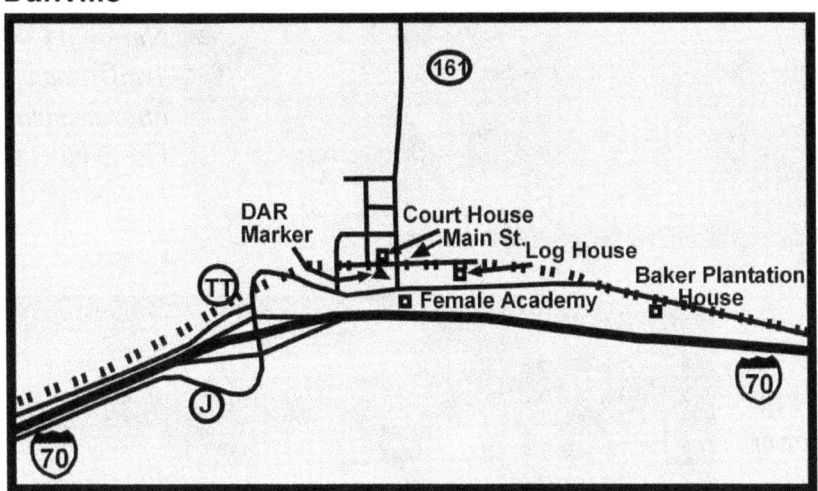

Stay on old US 40 and you come to the junction with State Rte. 161. On your left stands the only remaining building of the Danville Female Academy. Danville was a center for education in the 1850s, with at one time four schools, three for "very select girls," and one for boys. The Female Academy was spared from Anderson's torches because, so the story goes, the girls yelled out the window that "we're rebels." There are informative markers next to the parking lot on the west side of the building.

Chapter Five

Turn right onto Rte. 161 and go one block to Main Street, which is the BLR. You can see the DAR marker about where the original courthouse stood (before the Anderson attack).

Danville, platted in 1834 and the county seat of Montgomery County until 1934, thrived early on with a hotel, stores, and several taverns. Unfortunately, the railroad bypassed the town, leading to its decline; then, after the Anderson raid in 1864, Danville struggled; it finally lost the county seat designation to Montgomery City in 1934.

This is the Williams House from the North, the original BLR side. The culvert in the foreground is a National Old Trails Road improvement. Photo by Ron Kamper

This is the interior of the Williams House showing its log construction.

Go east on Main Street a block and you will come to the log house now disguised with shingles. The front of the house originally faced north on the BLR, but when US 40 was constructed on the south side, the front door was moved to face that direction. The logs are not visible from the outside but clearly seen when you are in the house. You must turn around here and return to old US 40. As you leave the house, you might notice a concrete culvert diverting water under the road. This culvert is a trace of the old National Old Trails Road, which was laid on top of the BLR. The culvert represents a modest improvement made when the National Old Trails Road was recognized.

Drive to the west entrance to the Interstate. However, go over it on State Rte. J, which becomes the south frontage road for about a mile.

G L O points

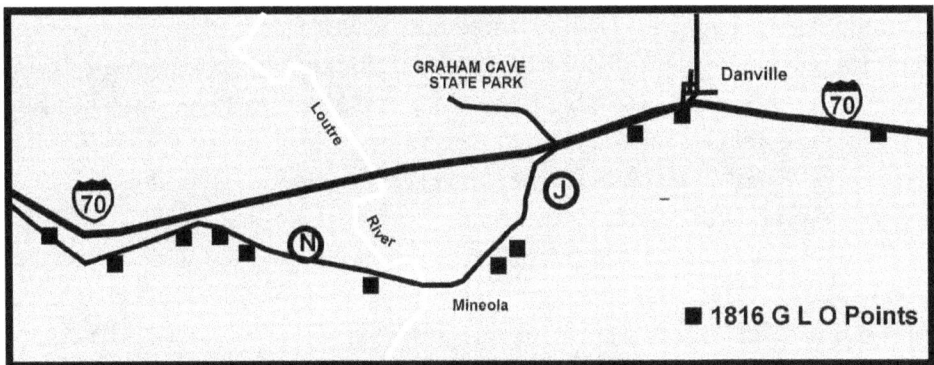

EARLY CHRONICLERS ON THE BOONE'S LICK ROAD

Early travelers on the Boone's Lick Road tell us much about the road itself and the people who lived on it. I have tried to incorporate the diarists' words when I can in this guide, for their words enhance the story of the road. Copies of these journals are not difficult to obtain, and I have included information in the bibliography that should help you find them. Your tour of the BLR will benefit greatly if you can read one or two journals before setting out.

One journal writer, Dr. John Mason Peck, was a Doctor of Divinity affiliated with the Missouri Bible Society. In the winter of 1818-1819 Peck traveled west from St. Charles, passing Kountz's tavern then descending to the Missouri. Unfortunately, most of his tour was along the Missouri River and not on the BLR. His journal has little to say about the BLR even when he reaches it, for he is focussed instead on a schedule of appointments he has made with a variety of settlers in Missouri. Peck's account does include much information about the Boone Settlement, however, as well as a long conversation with Col. Daniel Boone, who was in the last year of his life.

James Brown Campbell left Virginia in company with his parents, seven younger brothers, and household slaves in September of 1819. They apparently went west seeking a better living, and in this enterprise they had a great deal of company. Campbell, who had some training as a surveyor, practiced that vocation while residing in the Boonslick country.

Campbell's journal, *Diary of a Journey from Virginia to Missouri in 1819 and Back Again in 1822*, covers the entire period; but we will be interested in the Missouri portions, especially their travels on the BLR in 1819 going west, and again in 1822 returning east to Virginia.

Campbell's account details how the family leaves St. Charles on November 6, 1819, and heads toward Boone Settlement, looking for a location to "winter over." Not finding a suitable place along the Missouri River, they head up the hill and intersect the State Road (the Boone's Lick Road) about 20 miles west of St. Charles. From here, they travel on the BLR to Franklin and other nearby communities.

The family returns to Virginia in 1822 not being satisfied with their situation in Missouri. Health issues may have been central to their decision to leave; the mother and others were probably suffering from malaria and perhaps dysentery. Campbell's carefully written journal has helped me flesh out important details of the early BLR.

Shortly after signing the Adams-Onis Treaty in 1819 that settled the boundary issue between Spain and the US, Stephen Long was dispatched to reconnoiter the new territory under US sovereignty. The official journalist for the Long expedition was Capt. John R. Bell. Bell traveled overland from St. Charles, with Long, in 1820 going eventually to the Rockies.

According to his journal, Bell leaves St. Louis May 4, 1820, crosses the Missouri River, takes the "upper road as it is called," and beds at Pond fort. From this point, Bell describes his travel on the BLR to Franklin in detail, making this journal a must-read for BLR folks. Bell departs from Franklin May 14, but not before giving us a vivid picture of this remarkable and booming town.

In the fall of 1826 John Glover made a trip by horseback from Mercer County, Kentucky, through Missouri and back on the BLR looking for a place to settle. This he did, finally, in 1835, later becoming a wealthy landowner. On his 1826 tour Glover was looking for good land and thus his journal is especially valuable for notes on timber and springs. Having come from a forested part of Kentucky, he did not find the open prairies of Missouri inviting for settlement.

For our purposes, Glover's journal begins in St. Louis on October 12, 1826. He crosses the Missouri River on that date, follows the BLR west and then returns east, arriving back in St. Louis on October 31, 1826. The editor of the article containing Glover's journal in the *Missouri Historical Review* points out that Glover gives the cost of lodging, meals, and ferries in Spanish dollars. A shortage of American coin led Missourians to use dollars that were coming to Missouri from New Mexico on the Santa Fe Trail. Spanish dollars are divided into eighths instead of decimally, so we see Glover paying 62 1/2 cents to stay at McConnols in western St. Charles County. Our fading use of "two bits" and "four bits" is a testament to our former use of the Spanish dollar.

Loutre River Crossing (Mineola)

The section of the BLR between Danville and the Callaway County line is interesting for several reasons. First, the Government Land Office (GLO) surveyor mentioned the BLR in his field notes in 1816. Since only this stretch of the Road is mentioned, it is likely that in 1816 it the only section of the BLR that was clearly recognizable. The GLO locations on the included map for this section show us how closely the modern roads follow the old Road. Those early travelers knew the "best" way and made a road that followed their instincts. The second point is that the BLR you are following is about to descend and cross the Loutre River. Nathan Boone had the Spanish land grant that included the Loutre ford. An important salt lick near the crossing was also in his grant. It is no wonder then, that in 1808 when Nathan guided William Clark west toward the future Fort Osage, the Clark party crossed the Loutre here at Boone's grant.

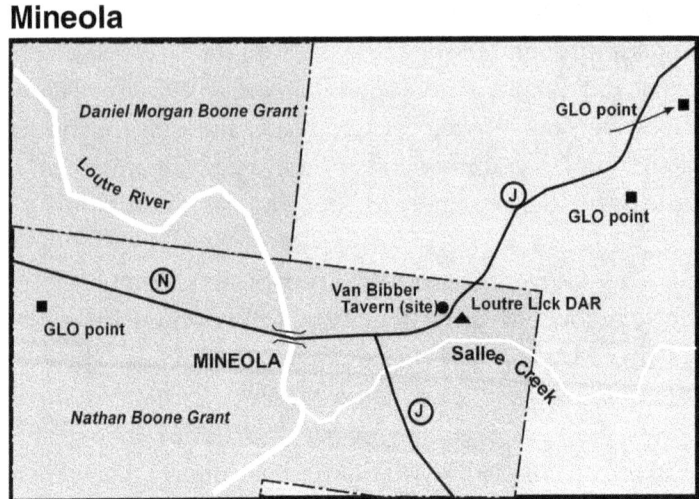

Map shows parts of the land grants of Nathan and Daniel Morgan Boone. A few GLO points fall in this area.

Most travelers mention crossing the Loutre about halfway between St. Charles and Franklin. They were following the divide between the streams headed south to the Missouri and then running north and east to the Mississippi. To avoid crossing the Loutre meant a very long detour north, so the ford here at Boone's grant was important.

Three accounts of crossing the Loutre are of interest to us. The first was that of Campbell in November of 1819. Campbell left Camp Branch early in the morning and wrote, "in a few miles we enter a prairie which reaches to the bluffs of Luter Creek, 28 miles from our last encampment." He makes no mention of a settlement at the crossing, so we assume Isaac Van Bibber had not yet arrived.

Bell, passing through Loutre Prairie in May 1820, writes, "left a Mr. Williamsons and proceeded, and at the distance of 7 miles arrived at Lotre Lick and put up for the night at the house of Col. Van Bibber." Note that it was the "house" of Van Bibber as it is unlikely that the two-story tavern that we know was there later could have been constructed between Campbell's passage, in November 1819, and Bell's stay in May 1820.

Van Bibber's Tavern

Van Bibber Tavern is shown about 1900 and not long before it was torn down. Courtesy of the Missouri State Historical Society.

National Old Trails Road

This photo shows a car ascending a hill out of the Loutre valley west of Mineola. This is the National Old Trails Road about 1920 and the photo is from the magazine that the National Old Trails Road Association published.

Bell also gives us a vivid description of the salt lick near the crossing. He wrote: "Near the house runs a creek, into which is placed, upright, a hollow log, 6 or 7 feet long, leaving about 2 feet above the surface of the water in the creek, into which boils up salt water, and runs off through a hole made in the log."

The lick is now under a gazebo near the creek and the DAR marker. The house to the right, north, side of the highway is about where Van Bibber's tavern stood.

Cross the river (the highway is now Rte. N) and continue up the hill. Note that the GLO section points are very close to the paved road you are on. If you look carefully, you may see some of the old culverts of the National Old Trails Road. Rte. N parallels the Interstate, and you will come to a spot where N makes a sharp turn over the Interstate. On the north side of the Interstate turn left on Old US 40, which continues as the north frontage road to Williamsburg. From here you are traversing Nine Mile Prairie, which continues past the next town, Williamsburg. You are also leaving Montgomery County and entering Callaway County.

Chapter Six

Callaway and Boone Counties

CALLAWAY COUNTY

The BLR from Loutre Lick west to Boone County was less used after 1822 so there were fewer sources to consult regarding its route. However, thanks to Ron Kamper, who learned much about back roads in Callaway County through his sixteen-year employment with Kingdom Telephone Co. in Auxvasse, I was able to discover the correct route. Ron sensed where it went, and I discovered a few journals that supported his view. I am confident that the route presented here is accurate. Remember "rules of the road": Stay on the ridges where possible and cross as few streams as you can.

Leave Loutre Lick, climb from the valley of the Loutre, and cross over the Interstate onto Old US 40, and you will soon be on the BLR. The BLR, from the time you leave the gallery forest of the Loutre until you reach Whetstone Creek, is called Nine Mile Prairie. Continue west on Old US 40 and, in about a mile after entering Callaway County, US 40 goes a bit north of west and you separate from the Interstate.

Chapter Six

Following Old US 40 west, you arrive in Williamsburg, where Missouri D comes in from your left. You are directly in front of Crane's store and the next-door Crane's museum. You parted ways with the BLR about one mile back (see map). In addition, you passed a DAR marker "Drovers' Inn 1836." The marker, after many years of lying broken and on its side, has recently been repaired and stands upright, though it is difficult to find because it has been placed back from US 40, on private property. It locates Drovers Inn on the BLR (also known as National Old Trails Road), which was a hundred yards to the north of US 40 here.

Williamsburg is a key location for the BLR. It was near Williamsburg that the BLR split after 1822, with the new roads heading southwest to Columbia, Fulton, and Jefferson City. Not every wagon used the new roads because the old road was still a shorter trip. Drover's Inn was an important stopping point for travelers. John Glover, in 1826 on his return east, wrote: "continued on and came to Mr. Truits where I stayed Tarried all night there I met with Mr. Walker and Mr. Polly." Mr. Truits was undoubtedly Alexander Fruit, who was here at this time. Both Alexander and his brother Enoch had licenses to operate taverns, according to Ron Kamper, but the tavern mentioned by Glover was on Alexander's property. Mr. Everheart owned the tavern at a later date, when it became known as the Drover's Inn, the first place the drovers could rest their oxen after the difficult trip from the Loutre valley.

Williamsburg

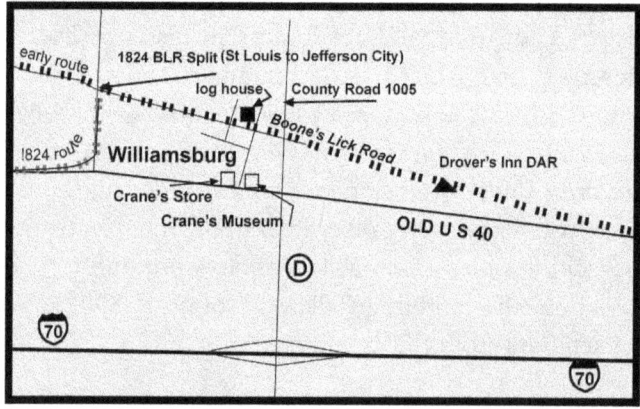

Crane's Museum is worth a short visit, as it is filled with items of local and national interest. The museum houses a nice café, whose customers gain free admission to the museum. The store, too, is worth visiting, as it was established here in Williamsburg in 1920 after having begun life in Mineola. Remember, we are on Old US 40, which was a major east-to-west highway from the 1920s through the 1960s.

Next, drive north on Co. Rd. 1005, the northern extension of MO D. This is the north-south gravel road just east of Crane's store that you passed earlier. In a long block, you will come to a stop sign, where the BLR comes in from the right. Turn left here and you are back on the BLR. One block west of this point you will find a house on your right that dates from the 1830s. The front part of the house stands parallel to the BLR while the back section, newly built, is perpendicular to it. The earlier section is made of logs, the most common building material in the early days.

Crane's house

The front part of this house is constructed of logs. The house sits on the Boone's Lick Road.

Drive west through the edge of Williamsburg to a crossroad and stop. In the early days of the BLR, until 1822, all traffic continued west from this important junction, headed for Old Franklin and the Boone's Lick Country.

Chapter Six

You will recall that in St. Charles you visited the building that served as the temporary capitol for Missouri while Jefferson City was being built as the state capital. In addition, Columbia and Fulton were founded about this time, and they needed connections to the east. All of this development meant that the BLR traffic began to be diverted southwest to Fulton, Columbia, and Jefferson City. From Fulton the highway went south to the new capital, Jefferson City. The corner you are at is the 1825 jumping-off point, the point where most BLR traffic headed southwest after 1825.

As you sit in your car on the BLR (also called the National Old Trail Road), you can see the next road to your south, which was US 40, an important road from 1920s to the 1960s, and beyond it Interstate 70, the latest highway in this important corridor.

THE OLD BOONE'S LICK ROAD 1816-1824

From this point, this guide will direct you along the older version of the BLR. In a another side trip, you can return to this spot and follow the later Road through Fulton, Columbia, Rocheport, and on to Old Franklin, or you can follow the route east from Old Franklin. That side trip is described after Chapter 7.

West from Williamsburg

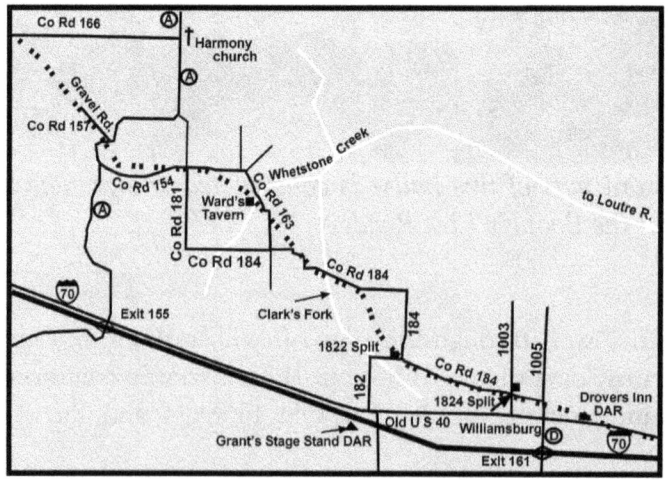

Continue west on Co. Rd. 184 (use the included maps) until you must turn right, at the intersection of Co. Roads 184 and 182. Remain on Rd. 184. According to local historian Kamper, at this turn the BLR split in 1822, continuing on to the northwest while Co. Rd. 182 became the 1822 St. Charles to Franklin State Road, passing through Smithton (later Columbia). Later, most travelers would turn west toward Columbia, whereas the balance would continue northwest toward Franklin via the old BLR. The map shows that when the road you are on tends to the northwest, you are directly on the old BLR.

You have been passing through Nine Mile Prairie since leaving the valley of the Loutre. Travelers sought the ridge between the south- and north-flowing streams, which route led them through a prairie nine miles in length. Whetstone Creek, which you will see, formed the west end of this prairie. James Campbell, in his westward trip in 1819, mentioned that few people were living in the prairies west of the Loutre. Later, on his way east in 1822, he writes that a Major Harrison and a Mr. Ward live on Grand Prairie. John Bell also says that in 1820 Ward was living 14 miles beyond "Lotre" Lick, which confirms Campbell's location for Ward.

PRAIRIE PARADOX

Early accounts of travel along the Boone's Lick Road do not mention taverns or settlements while the writer is traveling through a prairie. They mention, for example, Grand Prairie west of Williamsburg, but no settlers resided there in the earliest period.

Several factors may explain why settlers avoided the prairies. First, in the early nineteenth century farmers knew the soils were fertile but they lacked the tools to cultivate them. They instead utilized the woods, where they would cut the trees and plant their crops among the stumps. Next, especially in Missouri, came dangers associated with living in an open area. Indian attacks continued into the statehood period (1821 on) but another, bigger threat was fire. Fires were often started by Indians to improve prospects for hunting, and lightning also set a few. Whatever the cause, all feared prairie fires.

Chapter Six

The last, and likely the principal, reason was one of technology. Until John Deere invented his steel plow in 1836, farmers used either an iron or a wooden plow. Neither of these plows was efficient at cutting through Midwestern soil, which stuck to them, requiring frequent cleaning.

Additionally, farmers needed wood to build their homes and barns as well as for firewood. They chose locations along creeks on the edge of forests and prairies so they would have wood and could let their livestock graze in the open land. John Mason Peck noted in his 1819 journal while traversing Two Mile Prairie, "here are about a dozen families in log-cabins scattered along its border." By the mid-nineteenth century, farmers could use the new steel plows to attack the prairies of Missouri, Kansas, Iowa, and Nebraska.

Jim Harlan, University of Missouri

Drive north on 184 to a sharp turn to the west. Watch for County Rd. 163, where you should turn right, north. Again, you are on the BLR, until you arrive at Whetstone Creek. If the creek is running full, return to 184 and take the alternate route shown on the map. I have had to detour twice in the last few years because of high water here. Whetstone Creek was a marker between Nine Mile Prairie and the Grand Prairie, which you will now enter. Grand Prairie was about 22 miles in width, according to the early travelers.

In 1819 Mr. Ward owned the property adjacent to the creek where he opened a tavern. After you cross the creek and ascend the hill, the BLR would have been to your left. On his way east in 1822 Campbell mentions seeing Ward's house, and Bell says in 1820 he ate breakfast at Mr. Ward's. You are now on the Grand Prairie, which continues to Cedar Creek, the present county line between Callaway and Boone counties.

Once it passed the Whetstone Creek, the BLR bent west to follow the ridge between two other creeks. After you turn left on Co. Rd. 154, drive two miles to paved Co. Rd. A. Road 154 does not follow the section lines here and meanders a little, a sure sign that it is the BLR. Turn right on A and in a short distance, on your left, turn on gravel road Co. Rd. 157. This road is on the BLR but does not go through, so you will eventually have to turn around and retrace your steps. It is worth the short trip.

On returning to Co. Rd. A, turn left and follow it several miles to Co. Rd. 166. Harmony Church will be on your right at this spot. Turn left on 166 and drive west toward US 54. Road 166 will turn into Rte. T before you arrive at US 54. Co. Road 166 is straight for several miles, but when it makes a turn to the right and joins T, you are back on the BLR. When T straightens out later, you have left the BLR as it has veered off to the northwest again.

Auxvasse

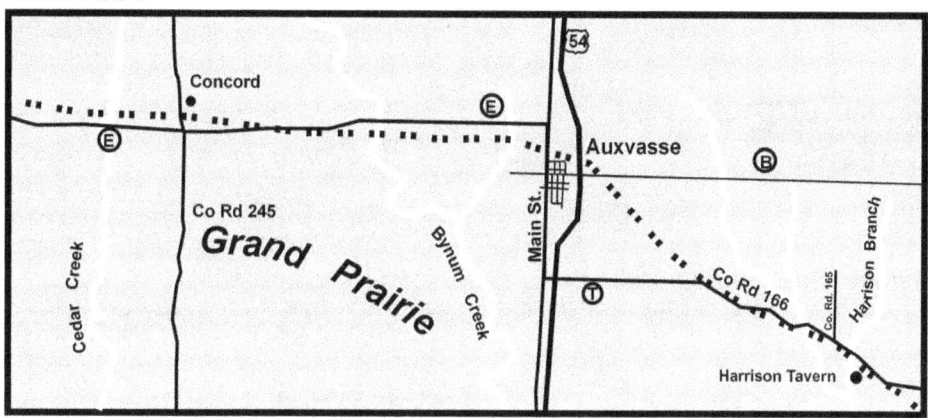

When you turn northwest on T, you come to a small creek, Harrison's Branch. At the spot where the highway crosses the creek, a tavern run by Thomas Harrison was located. Campbell called Harrison Major Harrison and said, "We proceed across the Prairie 22 miles to Major Harrison's where we stop about 2 o'clock and feed." Harrison bought land in December 1819 and must have bought the quarter section north of his first property soon after that, because the tavern was built on the latter piece of land. The Harrison Cemetery can be seen just south of the road to the southwest here. There were but two taverns on the Grand Prairie between Drover's Inn and Cedar Creek.

The BLR ran under Co. Rd. 166 (and T) as indicated on the map but angled northwest to pass through present day Auxvasse. Travelers used this little detour to avoid the worst section of Bynum Creek (tributary to Auxvasse Creek), which makes a deep cut here.

You will intersect with US 54, where you should turn north. Just north of Auxvasse, turn left onto Rte E. The BLR follows E almost due west for many miles. After it crosses Bynum Creek, E does not directly follow the section lines, a sign that the road was here first, before the surveyors. A few miles after leaving US 54 near a large rural water supply tank, you might see a few houses left from Concord, a community formed after the heyday of the BLR but when it was still active.

Western Callaway County

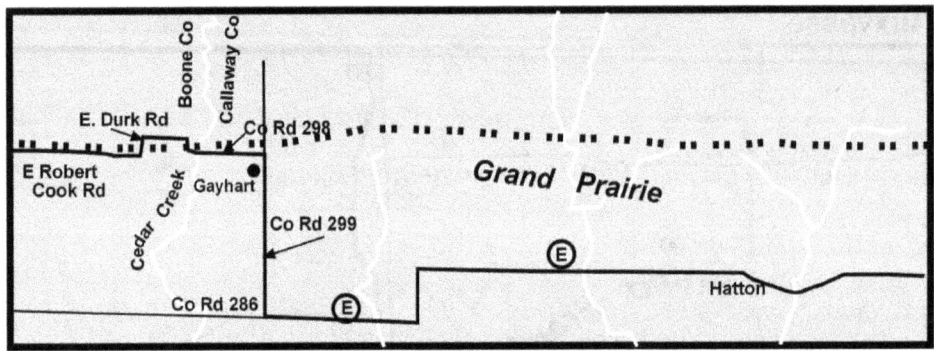

Cedar Creek forms the county line between Callaway and Boone counties and identified the western boundary of Grand Prairie. An entry in Campbell's journal helps nail down the BLR route in this vicinity. Campbell (on his trip east in 1822) wrote: "to Cedar Creek, one branch of which we crossed and encamp on another near the west edge of the Grand Prairie near Gayhart." Gayhart was really a reference to Isaac Gearheart, who owned land in western Callaway County in late 1818. His land is noted on the included map as Gayhart. The BLR probably lay about where it is placed on the map, but this area has been thoroughly strip-mined so the landscape looks more like a moonscape.

Follow E until you turn right, north, on Co. Rd. 299. Continue 1.5 miles and turn left on Co. Rd. 298, which will take you across the creek and the county line. After passing into Boone County, the road is named E. Durk Road.

BOONE COUNTY

Boone County has been thoroughly researched for all aspects of the early version of the Boone's Lick Road. David Sapp of Columbia spent many years looking at every record he could find and talking to any landowner he could. He also spent hours walking the route and checking creeks for BLR crossings. Sapp published the results of his work in his book *The 1820 Route of the Boone's Lick Trail Across Boone County, Missouri.* This chapter will incorporate his work with few differences but in much less detail. Sapp writes that about eleven and a half miles of modern roads are on top of the old BLR. This means about 50 per cent of the BLR in Boone County is still in use. We do have two newly found travel journals that help to flesh out stories at some of Sapp's locations.

Murry corner

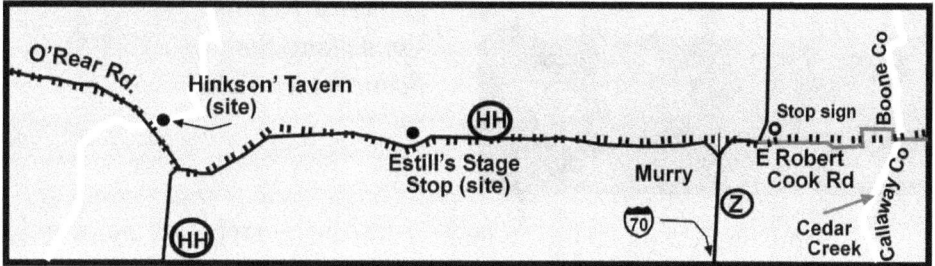

After crossing Cedar Creek, drive west from Callaway County on Durk Road, which becomes E. Robert Cook Rd. You will come to State Rte. Z and a place called Murry Corner. The BLR passes through the corner and you can drive into the triangular-shaped piece of land at the corner and see the BLR route. To reach the interior, drive north on the extension of Route Z, a narrow lane that dead-ends in 100 yards. Look east and west at this point to see the BLR. Return to Rte. HH and turn right. Reverend Peck called this section from Cedar Creek to Murry Two Mile Prairie when he rode by in 1819. He wrote: "It derives its name from its average width, commences between two points of timber towards the Missouri, and extends a long distance northward until lost in the Grand Prairie." Campbell, in 1819 and again in 1822, also mentions this two-mile prairie.

Continue west on Rte. HH for about 1.5 miles and you are near the location of Estill's Stage Stop. Route HH dips a bit to the south here, perhaps as a result of having to avoid the stage stop. Benjamin Estill came to Boone County about 1818 and opened a tavern here. By early 1824, when the property was sold at auction because of a judgment against it, much of the traffic using the BLR had shifted south, so it is no wonder the tavern failed. Both Campbell in 1822 and Bell in 1820 mention the Estill station.

The Boone County Historical Society has placed several of these attractive signs along the Boone's Lick Road.

Continue west on HH to an intersection where HH turns south. Take the road to the right, O'Rear, to follow the BLR route. Near the point where you cross Hinkson's Creek, a Mr. Robert Hinkson ran a tavern. Reverend Peck, who visited the tavern in late 1818, provides a first-hand account. He wrote, "the cabin was a single room of most primitive fashion, spice bush tea was substitute for coffee, and the flesh of hog, bear, deer, and elk was plenty …" He later added, "The corn-dodgers were cold and quite unpalatable; for the good woman had never learned the art of cleanliness and cookery."

Browns Station Road to Hinton

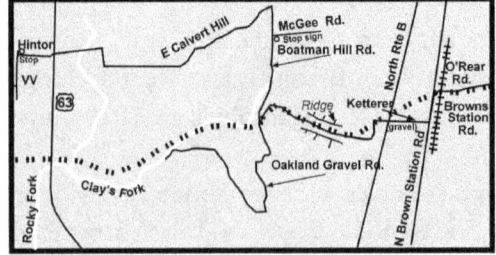

O'Rear Road meets N. Brown Station Rd. just after you cross some railroad tracks. Turn left here and drive south two-tenths of a mile to Ketterer. Then go right on Ketterer, passing a very busy Rte. B, and you will drive on a narrow ridge separating two stream courses. You will be on the BLR for the next two miles.

As you reach the bottom of the hill, turn right on a gravel road, Boatman Hill Rd. Follow Boatman, and continue on E. Calvert Hill Rd. to US 63. You have been north of the BLR for the last few miles. Cross US 63 and continue to a stop sign in Hinton where you turn left here on Rte. VV and drive south four-tenths of a mile to Akeman Bridge Rd.

West to Persia

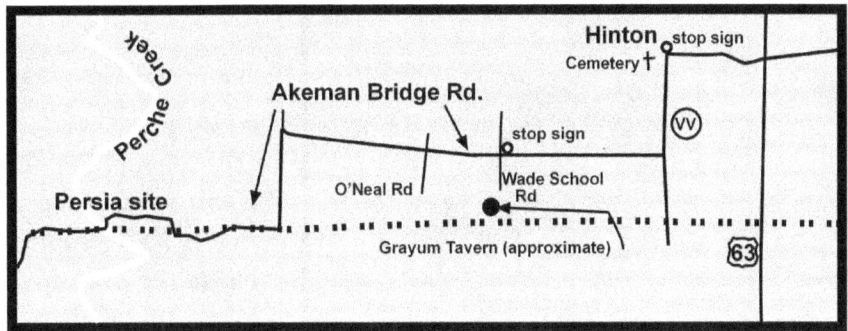

Akeman Bridge Rd. goes west before turning sharply south and then west again. After turning on Akeman, you should come in about one-half mile to a stop sign at Wade School Road. John Grayum operated a tavern about a half-mile south of here. Campbell mentioned the tavern on his way east in 1822, as did Bell in 1820. When you turn to head west again, you are back on the BLR. In a mile, you will reach a bridge over Perche Creek.

At this point, you are in the old "town" of Persia. Persia was platted in 1820, after the BLR was well established. Bell wrote of Persia, "it was recently laid out, on the bank of a creek of that name-we saw nothing but stakes driven in the ground to mark, I suppose, the streets of this new town..." The map in this section labeled "Old Persia" should give you some idea of the community, at least as it was envisioned. Campbell, passing through on his way east in 1822, is more damning than Bell. He wrote: "The Persia town is laid out on a hill on the west side of the creek; a number of buildings are

Chapter Six

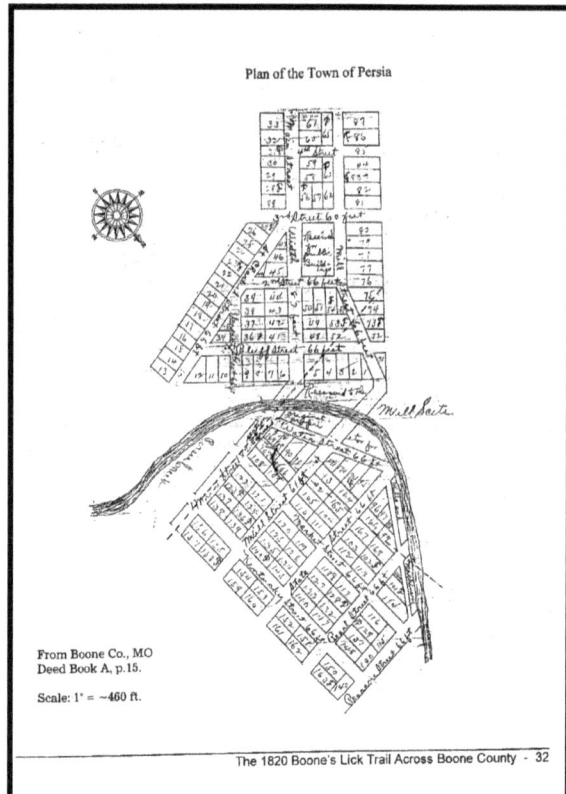

This is the original plan for the town of Persia. You must orient the map correctly before comparing it to the next map.

begun, the most of which are going to decay before being finished. It exhibits not so much the decline of the country as it does an artful (or rather fraudulent) speculating scheme accomplished by imposing on the sanguine and credulous who purchased lots at a high price."

Immediately after you cross the bridge at Perche Creek, keep a close eye to your left and you can see the old trail coming up from the creek at an angle. This would be "St. Charles Street." It never was much of a community -- just a few buildings and many dreams.

Continue on Akeman Bridge Rd. until you reach a stop sign at Rte. E. Drive straight ahead, on a road now called O. B. Brown. In about one-half mile, you will approach a very small creek. Just before the creek, on your left, are clearly visible swales of the old Sexton's Road that originated in Columbia and ended at the BLR. Sexton's pre-1820 tavern is thought to have been locat-

Old Persia

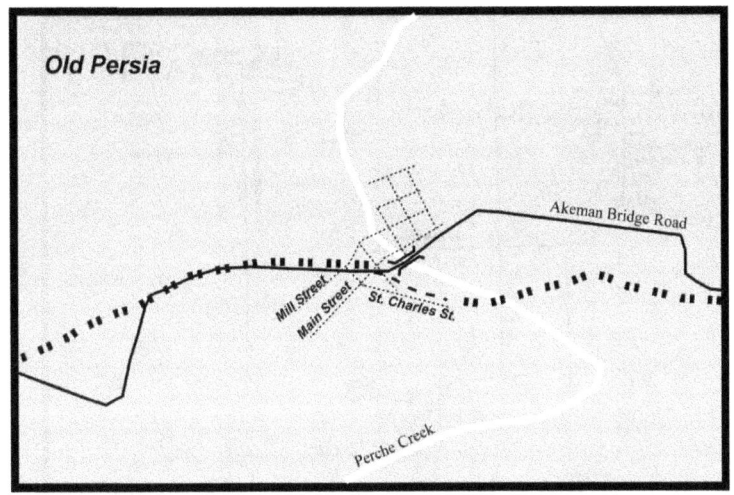

I have oriented this version so that north is to the top of the page. You can see "St. Charles St." here and compare it to the St. Charles St. on the previous map. That, of course, is the BLR.

ed on the rise southwest of this intersection, near where the more recent barn can still be seen. Bell mentioned "Saxons" when he passed through in 1820.

O. B. Brown Road swings a bit south and becomes Bell Rd. Follow Bell and turn left, south, on Locust Grove Church Rd. Just after turning south, look for Goodson Drive on your right. Take Goodson Dr. (it dead ends) to drive on the BLR. Then return to Locust Grove Church Rd. and drive south for about three miles. You must a make a large detour here in order to pick up the BLR west of the segment you drove on Goodson (see map).

Locust Grove Church Rd. runs south; after three miles you must turn right on Westlake Rd.; drive one and a half miles on Westlake to a stop sign. Turn right here on Boothe Lane and drive north one mile to Graham Rd., where you turn right and follow it until you see a white fence on the left. At the end of the fence, turn left and drive on the gravel road to a small creek. If your car is suitable, cross the stream and drive to the top of the hill.

Otherwise, park here and walk to the top of the hill. A short walk will reward you with a six-tenths mile stretch of deep swales. The county now owns this stretch and everyone is hoping that it will be developed for visitors.

Longest Segment

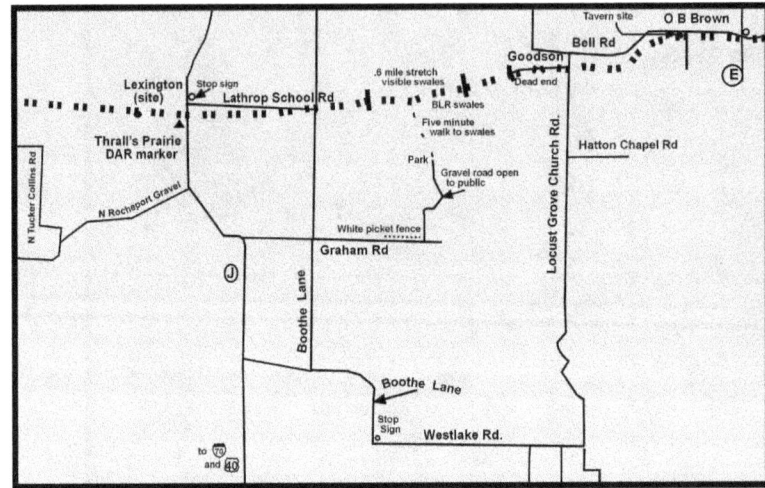

There may be some markers there when you visit.

I have suggested at several points in this guide that travelers used the older version of the BLR after more recent alternative sections were opened beginning in 1822. When I stand in these very large swales, I feel that they had to have formed over a longer period of time than 1816 to 1822. Dave Sapp tells me that the old BLR was in use long after the diversions west of Williamsburg took place. Sexton's huge stage and hauling business, which was located on the old road, was operating in the 1830s, and county atlases show

Ron Kamper is shown inspecting the swales that may become part of a Boone's Lick Road park.

the road in 1875. Many wagons did pass here between 1816 and 1822 but not enough to create these deep fissures in the prairie.

Return to Graham Rd., follow it to Boothe Lane, where you turn right, then travel on Boothe Lane to Lathrop School Rd. Turn left on Lathrop and continue to a stop sign at Rte J. Lathrop is mainly on the BLR.

Settlement along the BLR occurred in two directions. From St. Charles, it proceeded to the west and by 1812 had extended to about Pond Fort. On the Boone's Lick end, settlement was moving eastward and made it to about the present county line between Boone and Howard counties. Farmers out of Howard County settled where we are here in Thrall's Prairie, in a gradual expansion of the Boone's Lick Country. There is a question of when this prairie was first settled. Some say it was settled in 1812, others, this writer included, say after 1816.

If settlers were living at Thrall's Prairie in 1812, they certainly would have abandoned their homes and moved back west to Howard County and its crude forts. These were very dangerous times. The early date, 1812, seems to have come from a county history written in the late nineteenth century. These "histories" are notoriously poorly researched, relying mostly on the tales of the old timers.

Site of Lexington

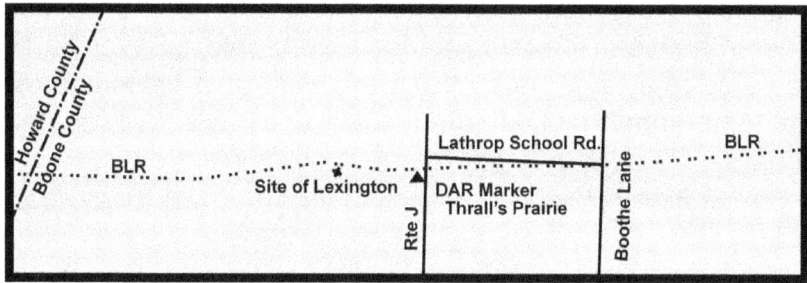

There was a settlement called Lexington with a post office just ahead of this stop sign. If you turn left here, you will see the first DAR marker since Williamsburg, on the west side of Rte. J. The marker, set in 1913 by the DAR, posts a date of 1812. Dan Rothwell's book *Along the Boone's Lick Road* uses both 1812-1813 and 1816 in his description for the area. Campbell stopped here in 1819 and noted, "there is a sort of town begun though not laid off. The land here is rich and beautiful."

Thrall's Tavern and Lexington

The high, fertile field a few miles northeast of Rocheport today is mute to nearly all evidence of the once bustling tavern stop known to all early Boone's Lick Road travelers as Thrall's. Armed, however, with a little local history and a sense of place, the curious onlooker can begin to see why the area appealed to the vanguard of settlers once the "Indian troubles" of 1812 were put to rest. The loess soil is amazingly rich and still several feet thick. The vista is open - all the better to spot a renegade band that might want to do harm. And if the onlooker trusts the red granite D.A.R. marker he can learn that the main road into the heart of Missouri territory ran directly across it, though today there is not a trace here of the old Boone's Lick Road.

This little patch of prairie appealed for all these reasons to Augustus Thrall and many others as early as 1817 and invited the first significant settlement in what would become Missouri's county named after the great frontiersman himself. Thrall's was a stopping point on the road just a day's ride east of the boom town of Old Franklin. Neighbors founded Bethel Church also that year, the first church between Cedar and Moniteau creeks. Oliver Parker opened a store and garnered the area's first post office commission in 1819, naming it Lexington after Kentucky's town of the same name. Though a bright future was envisioned by all in the area, competition for riches compelled others to vie for the same rewards.

A new county was to be formed from Howard County west of Cedar Creek. The jackpot would go to the county seat. The settlement around the Lexington post office, unfortunately, was too close to the likely northwest border and did not have the political clout to best the new, well-healed venture pushed by the Smithton Company. They even had the nerve to blaze a new branch of the main road beginning clear over in Callaway County to capture the westward traveler and eventually route him six miles farther south through what became Columbia. Parker felt the way the winds were blowing and moved his mercantile operation into Columbia. Others gravitated to either Franklin or Columbia.

The Lexington post office closed. The community at Thrall's continued into the 1840s but was more and more an outpost. Traffic on the road slowed as travelers favored the southern route. Eventually almost all traces of this vanguard community vanished. Recent archaeological work, however, has revealed the probable location of the once-busy Thrall's tavern as well as a nearby blacksmith shop.

Dave Sapp, President, Boone's Lick Road Association

A few words about this DAR marker are required. The last DAR marker you saw was for Drover's Inn just east of Williamsburg. The Daughters of the American Revolution marked the later version of the BLR that became the National Old Trails Road in 1912. This "new" BLR headed southwest from Williamsburg traveling through Fulton, Columbia, and Rocheport before entering Howard County. The first two DAR markers in Howard County were placed at Head's Fort and Arnold's Inn, both on the new BLR. So why did the DAR go east into Boone County to place a marker at Lexington on the original BLR? The marker says it is on the BLR. A nice mystery, I think.

Drive south on Rte. J one-half mile to N. Rocheport Gravel Road and take it southwest. This road wanders around a bit but eventually you will come to N. Tucker Collins, where you turn right. Follow N. Tucker Collins to West Drake Lane, go west on W. Drake Lane across the Howard County line, where the road becomes Co. Rd. 438. The BLR passed north of here, probably aiming for Big Spring (now not so big). Continue on 438 until it meets Howard Co. Rd 433.

Western Boone County/Eastern Howard County

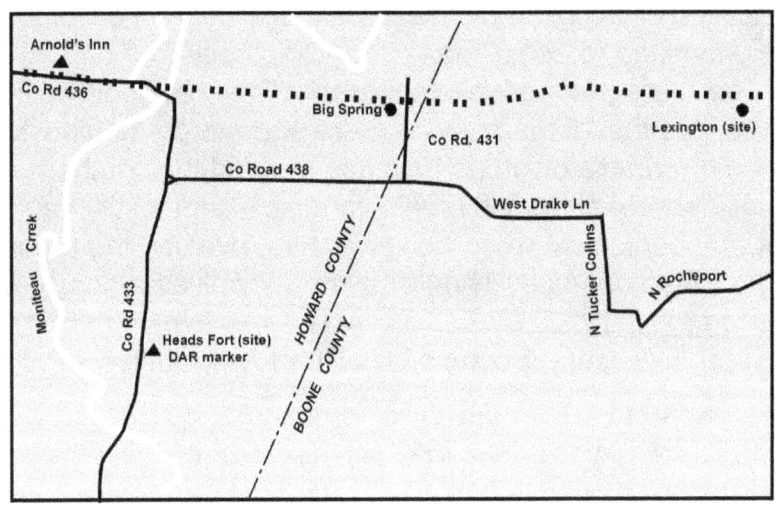

Thrall's Prairie

David Sapp is shown admiring the Lexington markers at Thrall's Prairie. The DAR marker here is inscribed "Boone's Lick Road," but this is on the older version of the BLR.

Chapter Seven
Howard County

The tour begins again after the following sidebar about Old Franklin.

Old Franklin

Old Franklin "Boomed and Busted" as few towns in the U S have. Only a few western mining towns had a fluorescence as brief as Franklin did. From 1816 when it was platted until 1826 when it began its death throes, Franklin grew to be Missouri's second largest city and ended with a few remaining buildings toppling into the Missouri River in 1829. The town had been flooded twice and the river channel ate into the town destroying almost everything. Early on, everyone who visited Franklin marveled at its growth and importance and predicted great things for this frontier town.

Settlement in the Franklin area began in 1805 when Nathan Boone, Daniel Morgan Boone, and James and Jesse Morrison began salt production at the famous Boone's Lick spring about ten miles northwest of the future town. The salt works required workers for cutting firewood, hunting game for food, and salt production. Keelboats took the salt downstream to St. Louis and brought supplies and foodstuff upriver to the salt works landing. By 1810 there was already a burgeoning settlement where Salt Creek came into the bottoms near the future Franklin in 1808. William Clark provides the first details in 1808 as he made his way west to build Fort Osage. His guide was Nathan Boone, so it was natural that the Clark expedition visited the lick and works. Clark wrote, "Continued through delightful lands to the Main Good Womans river..." This stream was, of course, the Bonne Femme River that runs a bit east of Franklin. Clark followed what he called the "high Bottom," which would later become the route of the Santa Fe Trail. It is the road just above the floodplain. He then arrived at "a butifull small plain Makays about a mile wide and crossed a Cart Road leading from Boons lick to the river." He also noted, "Some Corn is raised on the river." "Makay" is James Mackay, who had the first claim on the lick in 1797. The men had begun farming on a small scale to supplement their food supply.

Old Franklin Area

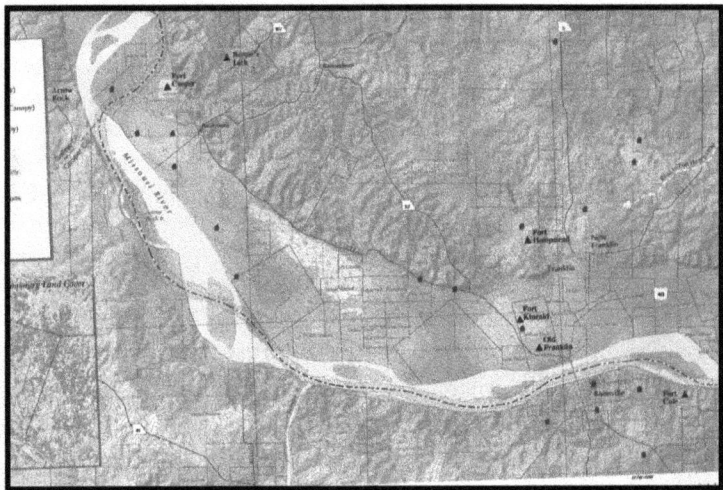

This is one of an extraordinary set of maps created by Jim Harlan of the University of Missouri. Jim used the field notes of the surveyors from 1816 to make a map showing vegetation and water courses as they were at the time. His original maps are in color and my black and white versions do not do them justice. He also has superimposed the land grants on the maps. These maps are available from the Geography Department at the University.

Col. Benjamin Cooper arrived in 1808 in the Boone's Lick with his family with the intention of settling. Cooper chose his land about two miles southwest of the salt works along the bottoms in the area that became known as Cooper's Bottom. Cooper's Fort was built on his property at the onset of the War of 1812. However, Governor Meriwether Lewis ordered Cooper to return downriver because Lewis felt that Indian claims had not been extinguished at this time.

Cooper and his family (wife and five sons) returned to the Cooper's Bottoms in 1810. Henry Brackenridge visited these bottoms in 1811 and wrote, "The bottoms on the N. E. side of the Missouri, uncommonly fine. There is a flourishing settlement here." He went ashore to visit the settlers and wrote, "We put to shore, at the farm of Braxton Cooper, a worthy man, who has the management of the salt works. The settlement is but one year old, but is already considerable, and increasing rapidly. It consists of seventy-five families, the greater part living on the bank of the river, in the space of four or five miles."

Shortly after Brackenridge's visit the problems with Indians became the central issue for the settlers. The War of 1812 led settlers to construct three forts in the Franklin area: Cooper's Fort, Fort Hempstead, and Fort Kincaid. From the location of the forts (see locations on accompanying map) it is clear that farms filled the Franklin area and not just in the Cooper's Bottoms. These forts would be home for the settlers for three long years as the war dragged on. A youngster named Kit Carson lived with his father and family in Fort Hempstead while young Josiah Gregg (author of *Commerce of the Prairies*) was living at Cooper's Fort.

After the war ended, in 1816, migration to the area began in earnest. The Boone's Lick Road opened in 1816 and by 1820, according to historian Jonas Viles, "the bulk of immigrants west used the Boone's Lick Road." Franklin was platted in the same year and Howard County was formed with Franklin as its seat. Howard County was reduced to its present size in 1820.

According to Viles, there were 97 lots in the original plat but this number soon increased to 678. There were two ferries along the waterfront and when Major Stephen Long visited in 1819 there were 13 shops, a sawmill, and a gristmill using oxen for power. Franklin's major attraction was its U S land office, which was located here from 1818 to 1824; it was the only land office west of St. Louis, so any migrant wanting government land came here to purchase it.

Long has given us our best first-hand account of a young Franklin. He writes that "Franklin was a growing frontier metropolis of 120 log houses of one-story, several framed dwellings of two stories, and two brick, thirteen shops, two large team-mills, two billiard-rooms, a court house, a log prison of two stories, a post office, and a printing-press issuing a weekly paper." The weekly paper mentioned by Long was the Missouri *Intelligencer*, established in Franklin in 1819. The newspaper migrated to the new county seat, Fayette, in 1824.

All of our early "journalists" had something to say about Franklin. Rev. John Mason Peck (in 1819) wrote, "At the period of our visit, no town west of St. Louis gave better promise for rapid growth than Franklin." However, John Bell's comments came closer to the truth when he said of Franklin that "its situation, and the uncertainty in the stability and permanency of these bottoms in high stages of water, must operate against the advancement of the town to a very considerable size." Bell observed that, by contrast, Boonville, "situated on a high bank of rock foundation in time will be a flourishing town."

The return of William Becknell to Franklin from a very successful trading expedition to Santa Fe in 1821 signaled a significant burst of energy for Franklin. The next year Becknell used wagons in his trip west to begin the Santa Fe Trail wagon road, and other traders followed. Since few steamboats were plying the Missouri at this early date (one boat in 1826 and another in 1828), we know goods destined for Santa Fe came to Franklin either by keelboat or the Boone's Lick Road.

In 1826 Bell's prediction about Franklin came true. High waters in the Missouri threatened Franklin but failed to destroy it. In 1828 Franklin was not so fortunate, as the Missouri roared over its banks and inundated the town. Residents organized and platted a new town called New Franklin two miles away on a bluff overlooking the bottoms.

Old Franklin's glory lasted ten years, from 1816 to 1826, followed by a sudden decline. Besides the threat from the Missouri, the trade from the Santa Fe Trail had shifted upstream to Independence. Thus, Franklin was not to be the important town envisioned in 1816.

Continuing west on 438 you will come to a Tee. (Map for this section is at the end of Chapter 6.) At this point (it is easy to miss the road to the north here) you should make a little detour to the left on Co. Rd. 433. When you turn on to 433, you have rejoined the National Old Trails Road, the first trans-continental highway in the United States. Driving south on 433 about nine-tenths of a mile brings you to the site of Head's Fort. There is a DAR marker behind a fence and hedge on the east side of the road here. Still visible, the white "spring house" was located within the palisaded walls of the Fort.

You are now on the later version of the BLR, the route that became the National Old Trails Road in 1912. The DAR, you may recall, marked the post-1824 route of the BLR. Head's Fort, named for William Head, stood at the very eastern edge of settlement before the War of 1812. Any settlers east of here were squatters, since the Government Land Office surveyors only completed their work here in 1818.

Return north on 433 past the Tee and you come to a corner where the road turns west on Co. Rd. 436. You immediately cross Moniteau Creek and then after about half a mile come to another DAR marker on your right, "Arnold's Inn 1821," just in front of the site of the inn. Since crossing the creek, you have been driving directly on the BLR and may see swales paralleling the road. Boone's Lick travelers used Arnold's Inn from the early 1820s

This is Arnold's Inn and it was located behind the DAR marker.
Photo courtesy of The Missouri State Historical Society.

until it closed in the 1870s.

Continue west 1.4 miles on 436 to the intersection with Missouri 240. Follow 240 to the right as it winds northwest, until it meets Co. Rd. P. Turn left at P and drive 2.2 miles to the site of Salt Creek Church on your left, where Co. Rd. 455 comes in from the south. All that remains here is the church cemetery. Founded in November 1818, Salt Creek Church survived until the congregation built a new edifice at Ashland, a few miles east. A DAR marker nearby commemorates the Salt Creek Church.

Arnold's Inn to Salt Creek Church

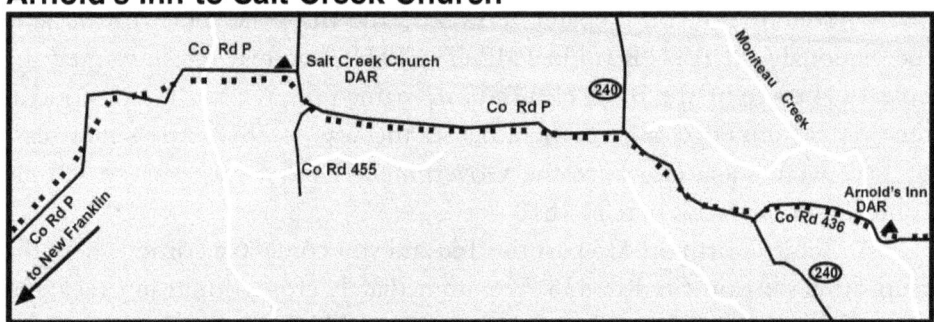

This photo shows a car at the fork where MO 240 and Co. Rd. P meet. The National Old Trails Road (or, Ocean-to-Ocean Highway) split here with one branch going to Fayette and beyond, the other going to New Franklin, Boonville, and Arrow Rock. This is the first trans-continental highway.

Continue on P, which sits almost on top of the old BLR. You will finally arrive in New Franklin on East Main Street. This town succeeded Franklin as the latter succumbed to a series of disastrous floods beginning in 1826. Many buildings in Old Franklin were moved up the hill to New Franklin.

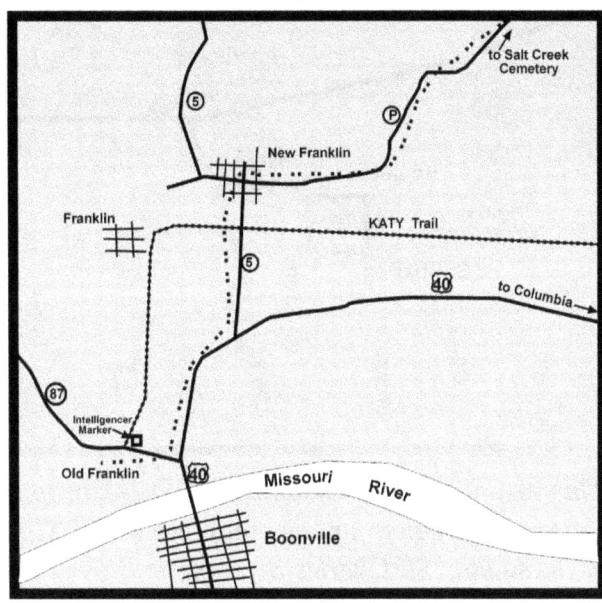

New Franklin

In the center of Main Street in New Franklin you will find a small protected area with two markers. The marker on the east side identifies "End of the Boone's Lick Road," whereas the marker on the west is dedicated to Franklin and the Santa Fe Trail. The BLR did not end, however, at this spot but rather on the town square of Old Franklin, at least until the 1830s. Likewise, the SFT began in Franklin on the same square, which you will visit later.

From the markers in New Franklin continue on Main to the intersection with Missouri 5 and turn left on 5. You will almost immediately begin a descent to the floodplain ("bottoms" as it is called here). You will pass the KATY Trail and then reach the intersection with US 40. Bend right here onto 40 West and continue to Missouri 87.

Turn west on 87 and drive a short distance until you see a small parking area on the right, which you should turn into. The KATY Trail is visible here, where it must make a detour, as the old railroad bridge is unusable.

Old Franklin

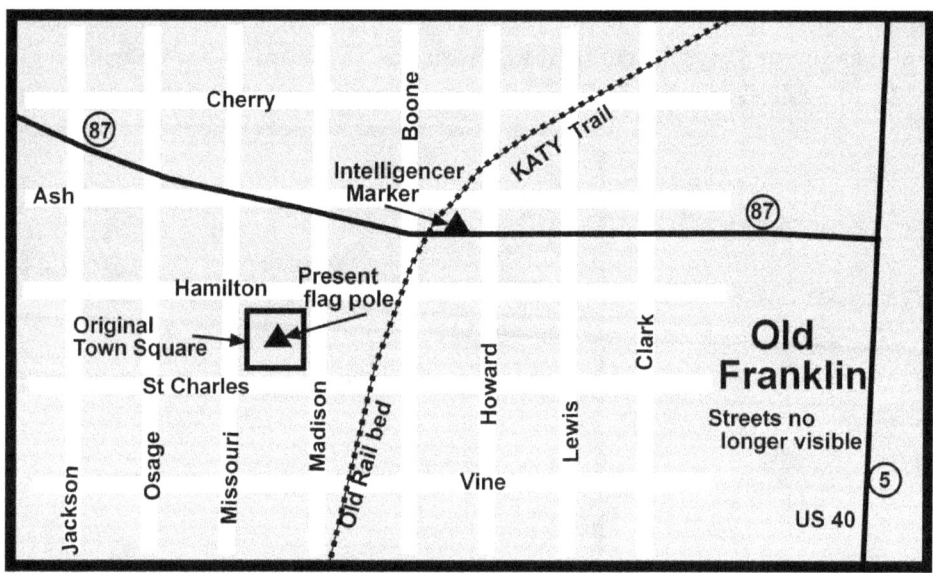

This map illustrates "downtown" Franklin in about 1820. Present-day features are shown for orientation. Note St. Charles St. on the south side of the square. St. Charles St. was the BLR at the time.

A few hundred yards from Intelligencer Park is this flag pole located in the center of the town square of Old Franklin.

The reason for stopping at this parking area is that you are but a block or two from the Old Franklin town square. You can see several important markers here, the most prominent being the one for the Missouri *Intelligencer*, the first newspaper published west of St. Louis, in 1819. Other markers locate Old Franklin and the Santa Fe Trail. In the very near future, another marker will identify the BLR. If you walk a few paces west and over the rail bed for the KATY, you will notice a flagpole in the center of a farm field that faces the Missouri River. The pole has been placed in the very center of the town square of Old Franklin by the Santa Fe Trail Association, who surveyed the site a few years ago. The owner of the land on which the pole is located envisioned a museum to celebrate the SFT and a steamboat that lies under the alluvium here. He hoped, as I am told, to excavate the boat and display it much like the Steamboat Arabia in Kansas City. The museum building can be seen off to the southeast of the parking area, near the river. It never opened.

From here, you should drive west on 87 to visit Boone's Lick State Historic Site. At about 2.3 miles from the *Intelligencer* parking lot, 87 continues toward Boonesboro, but you should turn left on Co. Rd. Z. You are on the Santa Fe Trail now and will observe a fine DAR marker on your right at eight-tenths of a mile. Dr. Horace Kingsbury built the attractive house behind the marker in 1856. The small brick Federal-style house attached to Dr. Kingsbury's home on the left dates from 1824.

Old Franklin to Lick

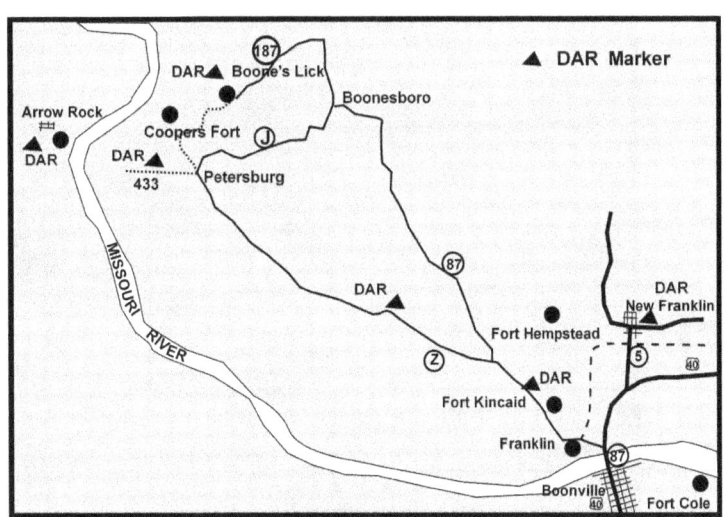

Continuing on Z, you see a small cemetery on your right containing the grave of Joseph Cooper. Beyond that, at about 1.6 miles, find a cemetery containing the bodies of Benjamin Cooper and his brother Sarshall, who was commander at Cooper's Fort during the War of 1812. One grave marker says "Sarshel Cooper" with a death date of 1815, but questions remain about his actual burial place.

Another .3 miles on Rte. Z brings you to the hamlet of Petersburg, where you should take the gravel road Co. Rd. 330 to your left and head toward the Missouri River. At about eight-tenths of a mile, you will see a DAR marker on the left for "Cooper's Fort." You may have to dig at the base to see "Coopers Fort," since when the area is flooded, silt sometimes covers the name. Just beyond, on the right, a commemorative sign tells about Cooper's Fort. The actual site of the Fort is not here but a mile north, which you will see farther along. Road 330, if extended, would take you to the ferry landing on the north side of the Missouri. Writing in 1826, John Glover says, "come on to Airy Rock Ferry at Mr. Becknal where I tarried all night. Becknal's house stands on the north Bank of Missouria on a Bank of sand 2 small cabbands bad appearance but good fair bill Ferriage and all 87 1/2 cents." We can't be certain that William Becknell's house was exactly at the end of this road, but it had to be close to that point.

Petersburg

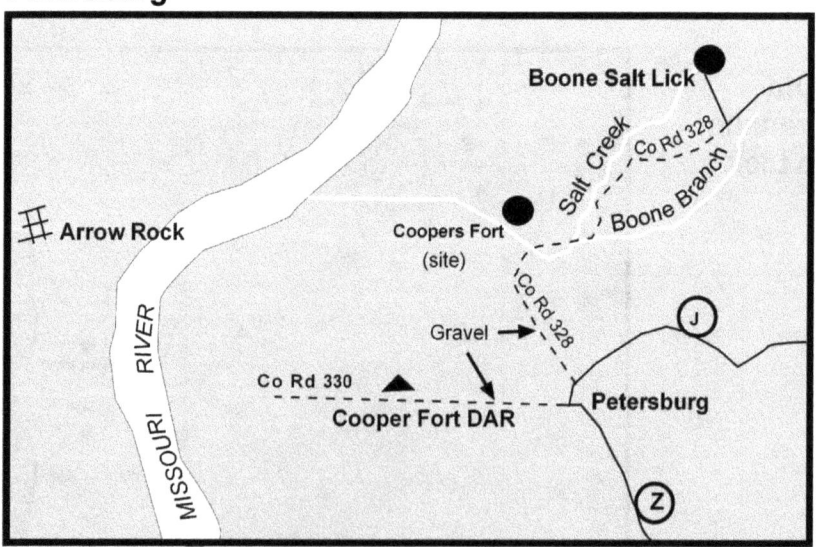

Howard County 109

Return on Co. Rd. 330 to the corner at Petersburg, turn left and left again onto a gravel road, Co. Rd. 328. Follow this road and in about one mile you will come to a corner where the road goes right over a creek and up the hill. Cooper's Fort was sited near the turn and about 100 yards west. Continue up 328, which will follow the course of Salt Creek. In 1808 William Clark wrote, "…passed thro a butifull small plain Makays about a mile wide and crossed a Cart Road leading from Boons lick to the Missouri." Thus, the first "road" in the Boone's Lick Country was a simple cart road used to take salt from the lick down to the river for shipment to St. Louis.

The Boone's Lick

The earliest commercial venture in western Missouri occurred at the famous salt lick in Howard County. This lick took on the name Boone's Lick after the two sons of Col. Daniel Boone, Daniel Morgan and Nathan, began a salt-extracting operation at the site. The salt operations of the Boones attracted many others to the area and soon afterwards this entire region became known as Boone's Lick Country, or simply "The Boonslick."

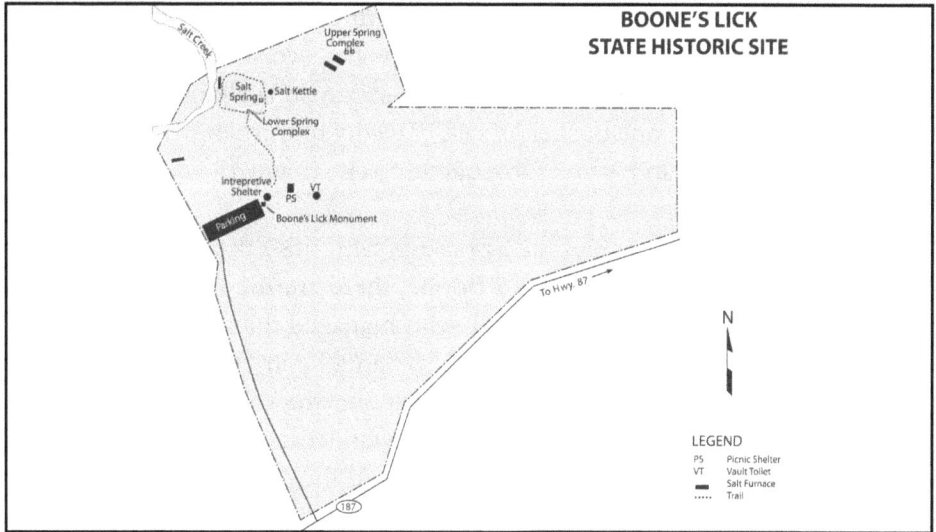

This shows the easy parking and access to the points of interest at the Lick.

For information about the lick, I rely on an informative article by Michael Dickey in *Missouri Resources*, a journal of the Missouri Department of Natural Resources. Michael is currently the site administrator at Arrow Rock State Historic Site and also administers the Boone's Lick State Historic Site.

Salt springs abound in this part of central Missouri. One county, Saline, is named for its many salt sources. Deer, elk, and other animals were attracted to salt springs and Indians would hunt these animals where they gathered.

Although Col. Daniel Boone was given credit by the DAR for the discovery of this lick, it is clear he was not the first European here. The lick was part of a Spanish land grant of 330 acres (400 arpents) made to James Mackay in 1797 several years before Col. Boone migrated to Missouri. Dickey mentions the problem of misinformation on the DAR marker at the site where Boone is given credit for discovering this lick.

In 1805 Nathan Boone began producing salt at the lick. James Wilkinson, then governor of Louisiana Territory, mentioned this fact in a report to the secretary of war. William Clark's journal of his 1808 trip west to establish Fort Osage mentions the "Cart Road" from the salt works to the river.

Production of salt involved placing brine water from the springs in large kettles, which were then heated on a stone furnace. Salt crystallized in the kettles as the water evaporated. Dickey says, "250 to 300 gallons of brine water was required to obtain one bushel of salt." Twenty to thirty bushels daily came from the salt works and were subsequently sent down the Missouri to St. Louis.

Some important names are associated with this salt-making operation. Besides Nathan and Daniel Morgan Boone, there are the Morrison brothers James and Jesse, plus William Becknell, who managed the works before heading off on the first successful expedition to Santa Fe in 1821.

This historic site is well worth a visit and the carefully planned walk has explanatory markers to help you understand the operation. There is a strong historical connection between this site and the early history of Missouri Territory and Missouri State.

Continue on Co. Rd. 328 until you reach the entrance to Boone's Lick State Historic Site, then drive into the site and park. From there you can walk to various well-marked points of interest. You will see a salt kettle among other items. The DAR installed one marker at the parking lot in 1913. Although the marker claims that Daniel Boone discovered the lick, we know now that it was discovered before Boone even moved to Missouri.

After visiting the park, leave the parking area but turn left at the entrance on State Route 187. Continue on 187 until the junction with 87. Turn right at the junction and follow 87 back to US 40. If you wish to take the side trip "Post-1924 BLR," you should turn left on US 40 and head toward Columbia. The side trip begins near Rocheport.

Side Trip on Later Version Boone's Lick Road

Between 1816 and 1822 the BLR followed the route described in earlier chapters making a sort of beeline for Franklin and the Boone' Lick Country. However, the founding of Columbia in about 1821 and Fulton in 1825 led to a shift south through these two towns. The first shift south came after 1822, when BLR travelers began to leave the earlier BLR at a point west of Williamsburg and head towards Columbia. By 1828 most BLR traffic went to Fulton and Columbia before going on to Rocheport and New Franklin. Remember also that the DAR marked this later version of the BLR, as it was the route used by the National Old Trails Road, also called the Ocean-to-Ocean Highway.

Columbia West

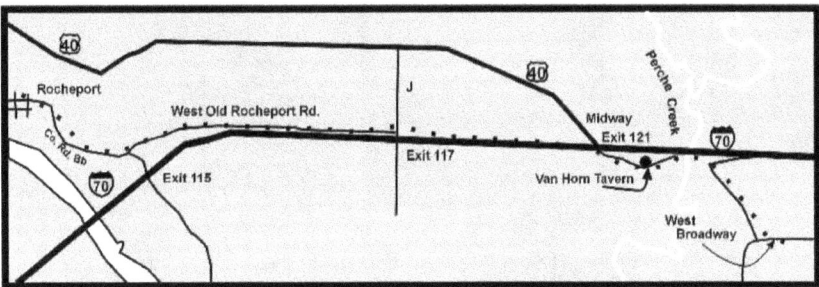

Drive east on US 40 from Boonville or New Franklin passing MO 240 on your left. Not far past the US 40/Mo240 junction is County Road 433. This road takes you to Head's Fort, which you visited earlier. The DAR marker at Head's Fort tells us that Co. Rd. 433 was on the later version of the BLR, the one the DAR marked in 1913. Continue east on US 40 four-tenths of a mile, where you turn right on Central Street, which is also MO 240.

You are now driving on the later BLR, and in one mile you should cross the Moniteau Creek, which is here the county line separating Boone and Howard counties. Continue into Rocheport, a small town that is delightfully situated along the Missouri River and the KATY Trail. In September, 1825, there appeared in the *Intelligencer* an advertisement for town lots in Rocheport. At about this time many goods destined for Columbia and western Boone County went through this river port. The DAR marker can be found on Second Street. Leave town on Third Street, which becomes State Hwy. BB. At 1.6 miles on BB, look for West Old Rocheport Road on your left, turn here and drive 2.3 miles east on the BLR until you reach MO J. Directly across J you will find a Missouri State highway yard and the BLR swales can be seen to its east. If you want to view them, drive north on J and then right around the complex and you will come to a large area in which you can park and view the route of the BLR. Interstate 70 is adjacent to the swales on their south side.

Van Horn Tavern

The Tavern was built near the crossing of Perche Creek, a bit west of Columbia. It was moved from its original site near the DAR marker to a position back from the road. It was converted into a barn with several additions. Now, it will be taken apart, stored, and finally rebuilt at the Boone County Historical Society Grounds. All of this will take time and who knows when the entire project will be completed. Photo courtesy of the Missouri State Historical Society.

Return to J, turn right (north), and drive 3.3 miles to rejoin US 40. Turn right on US 40 and continue east 3.8 miles to the intersection with Interstate 70 at Exit 121. Drive over the Interstate on U S 40 but do not enter the interstate on-ramp; instead, turn right on N. State Hwy UU and then almost immediately left onto West Van Horn Tavern Road. At about one-third mile, you will see a DAR marker "Van Horn's Tavern 1820" on your left. Until early 2012 the tavern remained at this site, but it is dismantled and stored for future restoration at the Boone County Historical Society. It is a remarkable dog trot tavern (recall that you saw a dog trot in St. Charles). Just past the DAR marker was the BLR crossing of Perche Creek. The Interstate has now cut off our access to the crossing and BLR.

From the Van Horn tavern site return to Interstate 70, take the eastbound ramp, and go east to the next exit (Exit 124), where you should get off and drive south on Stadium Blvd to W. University. West University is the BLR here, and it goes west for about a mile before the BLR turned northwest to head for the Perche Creek crossing and Van Horn's tavern. You should turn east here and drive on W. University. One interesting fact is that the later version of the BLR is more likely to be on section lines. The earlier version pre-dated the GLO surveys, so it tended to follow the best topographical course. The later version came after the GLO surveys, so often, as here on Broadway, the BLR lies directly on the section lines.

Drive east on Broadway and you will soon be approaching the downtown area and the University of Missouri campus. Columbia began life as Smithton and the DAR placed their marker where Smithton was located (established 1818). You can see the marker at the entrance to John A. Stewart Park, between the 200 and 300 block of West Broadway. The folks in Smithton moved east across the Flat Branch Creek in 1821 for a more dependable water source, and renamed the community Columbia.

Continue east on Broadway until you cross US 63 (the principal highway south to Jefferson City). The next DAR marker, "Vivions Stage Stand 1827," will be on the south side of Route WW (name changed for the extension of Broadway at US 63). Farther east, in Millersburg, is another DAR marker, "Millersburg 1829." This road is the old National Old Trails Road, so that explains the DAR marker.

The later BLR

At Millersburg the highway designation changes to Rte. F and remains F until the next important stop at Fulton. Fulton, founded in 1825 and named for Robert Fulton, inventor of the first steamboat, is worth a visit. One of its principal attractions is Westminster College, where Winston Churchill made his famous "Iron Curtain" speech in 1946. Be sure to visit the Winston Churchill Memorial and Library in Fulton.

Look for Rte. Z in the northern part of Fulton, which will take you back to Interstate 70 on the BLR. As you approach Auxvasse Creek, you will see the DAR marker "Jones Tan Yard" on the left. Tanning hides was an important job in the early days, as leather was used for all sorts of products. This area, known as Calwood, had a post office at one time.

Continue on Z until you reach the interstate. The route described in this side trip was part of the National Old Trails Road from 1913 to about 1927, when US 40 was built. It was not the only road used by travelers as they went west. From Williamsburg there was an earlier route (1822) to Columbia before Fulton was founded, a route still in use in many sections of Callaway and Boone counties. Ron Kamper says he has driven or walked its entire length. He says the break in the road came in the late 1930's when the bridge over Auxvasse Creek was destroyed in a flood.

NOTES

Chapter One

Page 1, "Were settlers": John Francis Bannon, *The Spanish Borderlands Frontier*, 1513-1821 (The University of New Mexico Press, 1974), p. 203. Both Father Bannon and Professor Abraham Nasatir cover the period before 1800 in detail. I have relied a great deal on the works of these two scholars. Dr. Nasatir was one of my teachers when I completed my undergraduate work at San Diego State College.

Page 2, " Father Jacques Marquette": Daniel T. Brown, *Westering River, Westering Trail* (St. Charles County Historical Society, 2006), pp.37-39. Brown's book covers much of the early history of Missouri exploration.

Page 2, "DeLisle published": Louise Barry, *The Beginning of the West* (Kansas State Historical Society, 1972), p.10. This is a wonderful book full of useful information.

Page 2, "de Bourgmont": Barry, p 12. Barry describes Bourgmont's travels up the Missouri River in detail.

Page 2,"Plains Apaches": Colin G. Calloway, *One Vast Winter Count* (University of Nebraska Press, 2003), p. 260 (note 203).

Page 3, "La Salle Expedition": David J. Weber, *The Spanish Frontier in North America* (Yale University Press, 1992), pp. 149-152.

Page 4, "Arkansas Post": Weber, p. 184. Weber thoroughly covers French settlement in the lower Mississippi Valley in the early 1700s.

Page 4, "Mallet brothers": Donald J. Blakeslee, *Along Ancient Trails: The Mallet Expedition of 1739* (University Press of Colorado, 1995). Blakeslee describes the entire journey of the Mallet brothers.

Page 5, "defensive barrier": Abraham P. Nasatir, *Borderland in Retreat*

(University of New Mexico Press, 1976), p. 2.

Page 5, "Villasur": Weber, pp.168-171. The fascinating story of this disastrous expedition is well told by Weber.

Page 6, "first experiences": Bannon, p. 193.

Page 7, "In marked contrast": Nasatir, p. 66.

Page 7, "in a sense": Nasatir, p. 34.

Page 7, "Canary Islanders": Weber, p. 203. The Spanish brought Canary Islanders to Texas earlier.

Page 8, " Fernando de Leyba": Nasatir, p. 23.

Page 8, "St. Genevieve": Weber, p. 202.

Page 8, " Kaskaskia and Cahokia": Nasatir, pp. 29-30.

Page 9, "Nootka Bay": Bannon, p. 225.

Page 9, "complete monopoly": Nasatir, p. 43.

Page 9, "the greatest of all intriguers": Nasatir, p. 36.

Page 10, "Nolan's plot": Bannon, p. 209.

Page 10, "population 1800": Brown, p. 132.

Chapter Two

Page 11, "1804 Population": Raymond D. Thomas, "Missouri Valley Settlements St. Louis to Independence," in *Missouri Historical Review*, October 1926, p. 20.

Page 11, "Col. Daniel Boone": Nathan Boone, *My Father, Daniel Boone: The Draper Interviews with Nathan Boone*, ed. Neal O. Hammon (University Press of Kentucky, 1999). Various pages from this book were utilized. Of the many books written about the Boones, this one is most valuable.

Page 12, "District of St. Charles": Jonas Viles, "The Provincial Period in the History of Missouri," in *The South in the Building of the Nation* (Southern Historical Publication Society, 1909), p. 196.

Page 13, "John Kountz": Kate L. Gregg, "The Boonslick Road in St. Charles County," Part One, in *Missouri Historical Review*, July 1933, p. 308.

Page 13, "several gristmills": Gregg, p.314.

Page 13, "rather the expression": Gregg, Part Two, in *Missouri Historical Review*, October 1933, p. 9.

Page 14, "a Pond at the out Skirts": William Clark, *Westward with Dragoons*, ed. Kate Gregg, (Ovid Bell Press, 1937), p. 21.

Page 14, "farm-to-market roads": Gregg, The Boonslick Road..." Gregg covers the evolution of the BLR in every detail in her articles in the MHR.

Page 15, "Our best reporter": See Henry Marie Brackenridge under Bibliography, and my sidebar on his 1811 voyage up the Missouri River to the Mandan villages.

Page 16, The interesting story of the Cole family is found in John C. Luttig's *Journal of a Fur-Trading Expedition on the Upper Missouri*, 1812-1813, ed. Stella Drumm, (St. Louis Historical Society, 1920), p. 31, note 13.

Page 16, "The Brackenridge Trip": Henry Marie Brackenridge, *Views of Louisiana with a Journal of a Voyage up the Missouri in 1811* (University Microfilms, Inc.), originally published 1814.

Page 22, "From March 10, 1804": John L. Thomas, "Some Historical Lines of Missouri," in *Missouri Historical Review*, October 1908, p. 230.

Page 22, "Private Land Claims": See Lamont K. Richardson, "Private Land Claims in Missouri" listed under Bibliography. Richardson covers every aspect of the very complicated issue of land claims in Missouri. In the early nineteenth century, Missouri had Spanish sovereignty, French sovereignty under guise of Spanish control, and finally American control.

Page 22, Pre-emption, a definition: the right of purchasing a tract of public land before others, given by the government to the actual settler upon that land.

Page 22, "New Madrid": Richardson, July 1956, p. 396.

Page 23, "Antoine Soulard": Over six hundred of Soulard's maps are available for a small fee from the State of Missouri. You can see all of them on their web site.

Page 26, "Jefferson's handwriting": Payson Jackson Treat, *The National Land System* (E. B. Treat and Co, 1910), p. 27.

Page 26, "Fifth Principal Meridian": R. D. Thomas, " Missouri Valley Settlements," pp. 26-27.

Page 28, "bloody details": Kate L. Gregg, "The War of 1812 on the Missouri Frontier," in *Missouri Historical Review*, October 1938; January 1939; and April 1939. Another of Dr. Gregg's scholarly works. A must-read for the period.

Chapter Three

Page 31, "peace arrived too early": Gregg, "The War of 1812 on the Missouri Frontier," April 1939, pp. 340-341.

Page 32, "highway into the interior": R. D. Thomas, "Missouri Valley Settlements," p. 22.

Page 32, Land survey GLO Notes and Index System: from Land Survey Program, Rolla, Missouri. Survey notes for counties in Missouri can be purchased from the above office. One can also purchase plat maps for each county. These maps were created from information on the GLO notes later.

Page 33, "Spanish grant": Nathan Boone's grant is shown on a map drawn by Antoine Soulard in chapter 2 of this book. If you look carefully, you will see the two fords, one of the small creek and the other of the Loutre River. The salt spring is also shown.

Page 34, "Isaac Van Bibber": Van Bibber's famous tavern has been imagined by artist Ron Kil for the cover of this book, from photographs taken one hundred years ago when the building was still standing. Ron's drawing shows an early stagecoach (pre-Concord style), a corral, and a blacksmith shop.

Page 36, "famous tavern": Van Bibber's grandson wrote an interesting letter to the *Missouri Historical Review* about his grandfather and the tavern site. It was published in the MHR in October 1912.

Page 37, "Boonslick El Dorado": Jonas Viles, "Old Franklin: A Frontier Town of the Twenties," in *Mississippi Valley Historical Review*, March 1923, pp. 269-282. Of the several Franklin "biographies," this one by Viles is the best.

Page 37, "During the month": *Intelligencer*, April 23, 1819.

Page 37, "12,000 settlers": St. Louis *Enquirer*, October 10, 1819, as quoted in Raymond D. Thomas, "Missouri Valley Settlements," p.36.

Page 37, "people were moving west": An interesting report in the June 9, 1819, edition of the Missouri *Gazette*. The *Gazette*, a St. Charles newspaper, stated that "emigrants were flowing through our town with their maid servants and men servants…"

Page 37, "frontier stage": Viles, "Old Franklin," p.277.

Page 38, "sales were dramatic": Sales figures are from Payson Jackson Treat's book *The National Land System*, 1785-1820, p. 409.

Page 38, "steamboat Independence": Viles, "Old Franklin... ", p. 269.

Page 39, "a plank road": Kate Gregg, "The Boonslick Road," October 1933, p. 14.

Chapter Four

Page 41, "one street": Henry Vest Bingham, "The Road West in 1818: The Diary of Henry Vest Bingham" in *Missouri Historical Review*, October 1945, p. 187.

Page 42, "it has but one street": James Brown Campbell, *Across the Wide Missouri* (The Borgo Press, 2007), p. 28.

Page 43, "vertical log walls": Dan A. Rothwell, *Along the Boone's Lick Road* (Young at Heart Publishing Company, 1999), p. 23.

Page 43, Sanborn maps: The Sanborn Fire Insurance maps give a broad picture of cities in the United States. The maps were made in order that insurance companies could have reliable information about towns they were asked to insure in. Information was on street width, building materials, and water lines. For St. Charles, there are Sanborn maps for 1886, 1893, 1900, 1919, and 1917. These are available on-line from the library at the University of Missouri. Columbia is also covered in six maps from 1889 to 1914.

Page 45, "Daniel Boone": For details of Col. Boone consult the side trip to the Boone Settlement at the end of chapter 4 in this book.

Page 45, "new marker": This marker is one of several you will see placed along the BLR and other sites. They are created by the DAR and have very accurate information on them.

Page 48, "Old Man Schaffer's": Rothwell, p. 30.

Page 48, "from Main Street": Gregg, "The Boonslick Road...," October 1933, p.16.

Page 48, "top of the hill": Gregg, "The Boonslick Road...," October 1933, p.16.

Page 49, "4 to five hundred Mormons": "The Mormon" in the April 13, 1833, edition of the Missouri *Intelligencer.*

Page 50, "Badly constructed": Bingham, "The Road West," p.188.

Page 50, "a rough, wicked": John Mason Peck, *Memoir of John Mason Peck*, D.D. (American Baptist Publication Society, 1864), p. 126.

Page 51, "Highway to Dardenne": *Westward with Dragoons: The Journal of William Clark*, ed. Kate Gregg. p. 21.

Page 54, "Encamped at a Pond": *Westward with Dragoons*, p.21.

Page 55, "constructed of logs": John R. Bell, *The Journal of Captain John R. Bell: Official Journalist for the Stephen H. Long Expedition to the Rocky Mountains, 1820* (Arthur H. Clark Co., 1957), p. 64.

Page 56, "Came to Mr. McConnols": John Glover, "Westward Along the Boone's Lick Trail in 1826, The Diary of Colonel John Glover," ed. Marie George Windell in *Missouri Historical Review*, January 1945, pp. 191 and 197.

CHAPTER FIVE

Page 67, "Hickory Grove": Nancy Short and others, *Milestones in Missouri's Past*

(Missouri State Society Daughters of the American Revolution, 1988), p. 13.

Page 68, "never hunted": Glover, p.197. Note 57 refers to Norman Pringle.

Page 68, "arrived at Jurnie's": Bell, p.65.

Page 70, "in a few miles": Campbell, p. 29.

Page 70, "Mr. Price's": Glover, p.191.

Page 70, "28 miles from our last encampment": Campbell, p. 29.

Page 70, "Jonesburg": Rothwell, p.53.

Page 72, "past the town of Louiston": Glover, p. 192.

Page 72,"bit of a mystery": I was standing in front of this house admiring it, when the owner, Ms. Leslie Williams, came out and invited me in to see the interior. The structure is best seen inside, where you can inspect the log walls and see the original form of the house. Many thanks to Ms. Williams.

Page 72, "built of logs: " This house may be the one described in the article "Life and Influence of Danville and Danville Township," written by Olive Baker and published in the *Missouri Historical Review*, July 1913, pp. 208-210.

Page 77, "Nathan Boone": You may remember the map in chapter 3 showing T48N R6W. Nathan Boone's grant was in section 34. The Soulard map of his grant is also found in chapter 3.

Page 77, "crossed the Loutre": There are two fords shown on the Soulard map of Nathan Boone's grant. One crosses the small creek coming in from the east; the other ford crosses the Loutre River proper.

Page 78, "bluffs of Luter Creek": Campbell, p.29.

Page 78, "left a Mr. Williamsons": Bell, pp.65-66.

Page 80, "upright, a hollow log": Bell, p.66.

CHAPTER SIX

Page 82, "came to Mr. Truits": Glover, p. 196.

Page 82, Alexander and Enoch Fruit: Ron Kamper located license applications for both Alexander and Enoch Fruit in the Callaway County Record Book, Vol. A, p. 36. The property on which the Drover's Inn stood belonged to Alexander. The name "Drovers Inn" came after Mr. Fruit's time when the tavern belonged to a Mr. Everheart.

Page 85, "Major Harrison and Mr. Ward": Campbell, p. 102.

Page 85, "Ward was living 14 miles beyond": Bell, p.66.

Page 86, "Mr. Ward": John Ward bought his one-eighth section in section 2, T48N R8W on April 19,1819. The only other early purchaser of land in this area was James Whitside, who had a quarter section southwest of Mr. Ward's.

Page 87, "22 miles to Major Harrison's": Campbell, p. 102.

Page 87, "Thomas Harrison": Ron Kamper found an application for a tavern license by Major Harrison in the County Record Book, Volume A, p. 25. Original land entries show Thomas Harrison with an early piece of land in section 32, T49N R8W. The date of purchase is December 11, 1819. To his north was a quarter section bought by Aaron Watson on December 16, 1819. The Harrison cemetery is on the Watson claim as is the likely tavern site. It is likely Harrison bought out Watson early as Harrison has many parcels in the immediate vicinity.

Page 88, "Grand Prairie near Gayhart": Campbell, p.102.

Page 88, "Gayhart": Original Land Entries show Isaac Gearheart with a one-eighth section in section 11, T49N R11W. He purchased his land here December 7, 1818. There was no other landowner nearby until the 1830s.

Page 89, "It derives its name": Peck, p.132.

Page 89, "in 1819 and again in 1822": Campbell, p. 30.

Page 90, "Benjamin Estill": David P. Sapp, *The 1820 Route of the Boone's Lick Trail Across Boone County, Missouri* (self published, 2000), p. 8.

Page 90, "Hinkson ran a tavern": Sapp, p. 9.

Page 90, "most primitive fashion": Peck, p.122.

Page 91, "Grayum": Campbell, p. 101.

Page 91, "Grayum Tavern": Bell, p. 67.

Page 91, "saw nothing but stakes": Bell, p. 67.

Page 91, "Persia town is laid out": Campbell, p. 101.

Page 93, "Saxons": Bell, p.67.

Page 95, "a sort of town": Campbell, p.30.

CHAPTER SEVEN

Page 100, "butifull small plain": Gregg, *Westward with Dragoons*, p. 26.

Page 100, "Corn is raised": Gregg, *Westward with Dragoons*, p. 27.

Page 100, the maps that Jim Harlan produced can be purchased from the Geographic Resources Center at the University of Missouri. Address is 17-19

Stewart Hall, Columbia, Missouri, 65211

Page 101, "The bottoms on the N. E. side": Brackenridge, p. 211.

Page 101, "Kit Carson": Josiah Gregg, *Commerce of the Prairies*, ed. Max L. Moorhead, (University of Oklahoma Press, 1954), p. xviii.

Page 101, "Josiah Gregg": Lynn McDaniel, *Bicentennial Boonslick History* (Boonslick Historical Society, 1976), p. 17.

Page 101, "bulk of immigrants west": Jonas Viles, "Missouri in 1820," in *Missouri Historical Review*, October 1920, p. 42.

Page 102, "120 log houses": Stephen H. Long, quoted in Jonas Viles, "Old Franklin: A Frontier Town of the Twenties," pp. 269-270.

Page 102, "At the period of our visit": Peck, p. 134.

Page 102, "the uncertainty in the stability": Bell, p.70.

Page 108, "come on to Airy Rock Ferry": Glover, p.193.

Page 108, "Ferry": According to Louis Houck, *Missouri from the Earliest Explorations* (Chicago: R. R. Donnelly and Sons, vol. 3, page 158), the ferry at Arrow Rock was established by Henry Becknell and consisted of two canoes lashed together with a frame on top and rails to keep livestock from going over. I gave this information to my artist friend Ron Kil and he drew the sketch at the head of this chapter based on that information. This method was common as I saw another reference to a similar ferry near St. Charles.

Bibliography

Baker, Olive. "Life and Influence of Danville and Danville Township." *Missouri Historical Review*, July 1913, pp. 200-223.

Bannon, John Francis. *The Spanish Borderlands Frontier 1513-1821*. Albuquerque: University of New Mexico Press, 1974.

Barry, Louise. *The Beginning of the West*. Topeka: Kansas State Historical Society, 1972

Bell, John R. *The Journal of Captain John Bell: Official Journalist for the Stephen H. Long Expedition to the Rocky Mountains, 1820*. Glendale, California: Arthur H. Clark Co., 1957.

Bingham, Henry Vest. *"The Road West in 1818: The Diary of Henry Vest Bingham."* Ed. Marie George Windell. Missouri Historical Review, October 1945, pp. 174-204.

Blakeslee, Donald J. *Along Ancient Trails: The Mallet Expedition of 1739*. Niwot, Colorado: University Press of Colorado, 1995.

Boone, Nathan, and Olive Van Bibber Boone. *My father, Daniel Boone: The Draper Interviews with Nathan Boone*. Ed. Neal Hammon. Lexington, Kentucky: University Press of Kentucky, 1999.

Brackenridge, Henry Marie. *Views of Louisiana with a Journal of a Voyage up the Missouri River in 1811*. Ann Arbor: University Microfilms, Originally published 1814.

Brown, Daniel T. *Westering River, Westering Trail*. St. Charles: St. Charles County Historical Society, 2006.

Burt, Huron. "Van Bibber Tavern,", *Missouri Historical Review*, January 1913, pp. 106-107.

Calloway, Colin G. *One Vast Winter Count*. Lincoln: University of Nebraska Press, 2003.

Campbell, James Brown. *Across the Wide Missouri*. Eds. Mary and Michael Burgess. Lexington, Kentucky: The Borgo Press, 2007.

Clark, William. *Westward with Dragoons*. Ed. Kate L. Gregg. Fulton, Missouri: Ovid Bell Press, 1917.

Davis, H. Denny. "Franklin: Cradle of the Trade," *Wagon Tracks*, May, 1993, pp. 11-17.

Ehlmann, Steve. Crossroads: *A History of St. Charles County, Missouri*. St. Charles: Lindenwood University Press, 2004.

Glover, John. "Westward Along the Boone's Lick Trail in 1826: The Diary of Colonel John Glover," ed. Marie George Windell. *Missouri Historical Review*, January, 1945, pp. 184-199.

Gregg, Josiah. *Commerce of the Prairies*. Ed. Max Moorhead. Norman: University of Oklahoma Press, 1954.

Gregg, Kate L. "The Boonslick Road in St. Charles County." *Missouri Historical Review*, July 1933, pp. 307-314, and October 1933, pp. 9-16.

Gregg, Kate L. "The War of 1812 on the Missouri Frontier." *Missouri Historical Review*, October 1938, pp. 3-22; January 1939, pp.184-202; and April 1939, pp. 326-348.

Houck, Louis. *A History of Missouri from the Earliest Explorations.* Chicago: R. R. Donnelley and Sons Company, 1908.

Levens, Henry C. and Nathanial M. Drake. *A History of Cooper County.* No location: Perrin and Smith, Steam Book and Job Printers, 1876.

Luttig, John C. *Journal of a Fur-Trading Expedition on the Upper Missouri, 1812-1813.* Ed. Stella Drumm. St. Louis: Missouri Historical Society, 1920.

Mc Daniel, Lynn. *Bicentennial Boonslick History*. Boonslick, Missouri: Missouri Historical Society, 1976.

Nasatir, Abraham P. *Borderland in Retreat.* Albuquerque:University of New Mexico Press, 1976.

Paullin, Charles. *Atlas of the Historical Geography of the United States.* Ed. John K. Wright. Washington D. C.: Carnegie Institution of Washington, 1932.

Peck, John Mason. *Memoir of John Mason Peck, D. D.* Ed. Rufus Babcock. No location:American Baptist Publication, 1864.

Richardson, Lemont K. "Private Land Claims in Missouri," *Missouri Historical Review,* January 1956, pp. 132-144; April 1956, pp. 271-286; and July 1956, pp. 387-399.

Rothwell, Dan A. *Along the Boone's Lick Road.* No location: Young at Heart Publishing Company, 1999.

Sapp, David P. *The 1820 Route of the Boone's Lick Trail Across Boone County, Missouri.* Self published, 2000.

Short, Nancy, Louise Taraba, and Rolfe Teague. *Milestones in Missouri's Past.* No location: Missouri State Society of Daughters of the American Revolution, 1988.

Switzer, W. F. *History of Missouri.* St. Louis: C. R. Barns, 1879.

Thomas, John L. "Some Historical Lines in Missouri." *Missouri Historical Review,* October 1908, pp.5-33, and April 1909, pp. 210-232.

Thomas, Raymond D. "Missouri Valley Settlements St. Louis to Independence." *Missouri Historical Review*, October 1926, pp. 19-40.

Treat, Payson Jackson. *The National Land System, 1785-1820.* New York: E. B. Treat and Company, 1910.

Viles, Jonas. "Missouri in 1820." *Missouri Historical Review,* October 1920, pp. 36-52.

Viles, Jonas. "Old Franklin: A Frontier Town of the Twenties." *Mississippi Valley Historical Review,* March 1923, pp. 269-282.

Viles, Jonas. "The Provincial Period in the History of Missouri," in *The South in the Building of the Nation.* Richmond, Virginia: The Southern Historical Publication Society,1909.

Weber, David J. *The Spanish Frontier in North America.* New Haven: Yale University Press, 1992.

INDEX

Page numbers in bold type indicate maps.

Acadians, 7
Alta California, 9
Alta Louisiana, 8
Anderson, William "Bloody Bill", 72
Apaches, 2
Appalachians, 8
Arkansas Post, 4
Arnold's Inn, 97, 103
Arrow Rock State Park, 34
Arrow Rock, 28
Astor group, 17
Auxvasse Creek, 116
Auxvasse, 87, 88
Baily, 55
Baker Plantation House, 72
Baker, Sylvester, 72
Baldridge, Milciah, 14, 15
Baldridges, 13
Base lines, 25, 33
Becknell, William, 32, 102, 108, 110
Bell, John R., 55, 68, 76, 80, 85, 86, 90, 91, 93, 102
Bethel Church, 96
Bingham, Henry Vest, 41, 50
Blanchette Creek, 13, 42, 43, 48
Blanchette Mill, 43
Blanchette, Louis, 13, 43
Blount, William, 10
Boat House, Lewis and Clark, 48
Bonne Femme River, 100
Boone County, 81, 89-98
Boone family, 11
Boone Monument and Burial Site, 64
Boone Settlement, 10, 12, 15, 18, 45, 49, 55, 56, 57-65, 76
Boone Trail, 14, 15
Boone, Col. Daniel 1, 11, 12, 15, 45, 57, 58, 59, 61, 64, 65, 76, 109, 110
Boone, Daniel Morgan, 99, 109
Boone, Nathan, 1, 14, 15, 16, 32, 36, 55, 60, 61, 62, 77, 99 100, 109, 110
Boone's Lick Country, 13, 31, 32, 34, 38, 40, 45, 83, 95, 113
Boone's Lick Road, 1, 32-36 (defined)
Boone's Lick State Historic Site, 107, 109
Boone's Lick, 16, 20, 23
Boone's Trace, 32
Boonesboro, 107,
Boonslick El Dorado, 37
Boonville, 16, 48, 113
Bourgmont, Etienne Veniard de, 2, 5
Brackenridge Travels, 17
Brackenridge, Henry, 15, 16-21, 101
Bradbury, John, 21
Bryan (Boone), Rebecca, 61, 63, 65
Bryan Cemetery, 64
Bryan, Jonathan, 61
Bryans, 58
Buchanans, 58
Burr, Aaron, 9

Bynum Creek, 87, 88
Cahokia, 8, 9
California, 39
Callaway County, 19, 80, 81-88, 88, 96
Callaway, Captain James, 31
Callaway, Flanders, 60, 61, 64
Callaways, 11, 58
Calwood, 116
Camp Branch, 70, 78
Campbell, James Brown, 42, 52,70, 76, 78, 85, 86, 87, 88, 89, 90, 91, 95
Canary Islanders, 7
Carson, Kit, 101
Carter-Rice Building, 44
Castlio's Fort, 29
Cedar Creek, 86, 87, 88, 89, 96
Central School Road, 50
Centuriation, 26
Chain, 34
Charrette, 10, 13, 15, 19, 31
Chihuahua (Mexico). 5
Chouteau Mill, 14
Chouteau, Auguste, Sr., 22
Churchill, Winston, 116
Clamorgan, Jacques, 22
Clark, George Rogers, 8
Clark, William, 14, 28, 32, 45, 54, 77, 100, 109, 110
Clark's Route West, 14
Clays, 58
Cole, Hannah, 16
Cole, Stephen, 16
Columbia, 36, 37
Columbia, 82, 84, 97, 113

Concord, 88
Cooper, Benjamin, 15, 101, 108
Cooper, Braxton, 20, 101
Cooper, Joseph, 108
Cooper, Sarshall, 29, 108
Cooper's Bottom, 101
Cooper's Fort, 29, 101, 108, 109
Cote sans Dessein. 15, 20, 31
Cottle, Warren, 51, 53
Cottles, 13
Cottleville, 49, 51
Crane's store and museum, 82, 83
Cross Keys Tavern, 70
Daniel Boone Trail, 64
Daniel Morgan Boone's Fort, 29
Danville Female Academy, 73
Danville, 72, 73
Dardenne Creek, 13, 14, 15, 51, 42, 54, 68
Dardenne Prairie, 54
Dardenne, 40, 51
Daughters of the American Revolution, 40, 46, 97
de Leyba, Lt. Governor Fernando, 8
De Ulloa, Antonio, 6
Declaration of Independence, 8
Deere, John, 86
Defiance, 19, 49, 64
d'Eglise, Jacques, 7
DeLisle, Guillaume, 2, 3
Dickey, Mike, 110
District of St. Charles, 11, 12
Dog trot house, 46, 72
Drovers' Inn, 82, 87, 97
Easton, Rufus, 22

Equinoctial line, 21
Estill, Benjamin, 90
Estill's Stage Stop, 89
Everheart, Mr., 82
Femme Osage area, 31
Femme Osage Creek, 12, 15, 45, 57
Field notes, 35
Fifth Principal Meridian, 25, 25-27, 32, 33, 56
Filibusters, 10
First Capitol Building, 46
Foristell, 40
Fort Hempstead, 101
Fort Kincaid, 101
Fort Osage, 20, 28, 45, 77, 100
Forty-second parallel, 9
Fox (Indians), 24, 25, 29, 60
Franklin. 13, 25, 27, 37, 38, 48, 76, 78, 83, 84, 85, 96, 97, 100, 102, 105, 113
Fruit, Alexander, 82
Fruit, Enoch, 82
Fulton, 37, 82, 84, 97, 116
Gasconade River, 19
Gearheart, Isaac, 88
Gill House Millstones, 52
Gill, John, 52
GlO Surveys, 33
Glover, John, 56, 68, 72, 77, 82, 108
Government Land Office (GLO), 32, 35, 56, 77
Grand Prairie, 85, 88
Grand riviere des Emisourites, 2
Gratiot, Charles, 22
Grayum, John, 91

Gregg, Josiah, 101
Gregg, Kate, 13, 28, 31, 48
Gristmill, 13
Halls, 58
Harlan, Jim, 100
Harmony Church, 87
Harrison Cemetery, 87
Harrison, Major Thomas, 85, 87
Hawk Ridge Road, 54
Hays, 12
Hayses, 58
Head, William, 103
Head's Fort, 97, 103, 113
Hickory Grove Prairie, 67
Hickory Grove, 56
Highway to Dardenne, 51
Hinkson Creek, 90
Hinkson, Robert, 90
Hoffmans, 13
Howard County, 1, 13, 15, 24, 25, 29, 37, 38, 45, 46, 49, 95, 97, 99-111
Howell, John, 14, 15
Hudson Bay, 6
Hunt, Wilson, 17
Independence, 49, 102
Iowa (Indians), 24
Isle a la Loutre. 19
Isle aux Boeufs, 19
Isle de Orleans, 5
Jackson County, 45, 49
Jefferson City, 42, 82, 84
Jefferson, Thomas, 10, 25
Jolliet, Louis, 2
Jonesburg, 70, 71
Journey, James, 68

Judgment Tree Park, 63
Judgment Tree, 61
Kamper, Ron, 81, 85, 116
Kansas City, 107
Kansas Indians, 21
Kaskaskia, 8
KATY Trail, 105, 107, 113
KATY Trail, 48, 63, 64
Keelboat, 15, 16, 17, 20, 32, 38
Keelboats, 99
Kennedy, Thomas. 67
Kennedy's Fort, 29, 67
Kenner, Rodman, 56
Kenners Tavern 1819, 56
Kentucky, 8, 10, 12, 37
Kickapoo (Indians), 29
Kingsbury, Horace, 107
Kiowas, 2
Kountz Fort, 29, 50
Kountz, John, 13
Kountz, Nicholas, 13, 50
La Charrette (also Charrette), 64
Labeaume, Louis, 22
Laclede, Pierre, 8
Lamine River, 15, 20
Land grants, 11
Land issues, 11
Land office, 25
LaSalle, Robert Cavelier, 2, 3, 5
Latter Day Saints, 48
Lewis, Meriwether, 15, 72, 101
Lewiston, 72
Lexington, 95, 96
Links, 34
Lisa, Manuel, 17

Little Osages. 21
Little Tavern Creek, 19
Long, Stephen, 16, 55, 76, 101
Loutre Island, 15, 19, 31
Loutre Lick, 36, 81
Loutre Prairie, 70
Loutre River, 32, 36, 51, 77
Loutre Valley, 82
Mackay, James, 22, 24, 60, 100, 110
Main Street, 41, 42
Mallet brothers, 4
Mandan villages, 6, 7, 21
Marquette, Father Jacques, 2
Marthasville Road, 14
Marthasville, 15, 19, 49, 60, 61, 63
Matagorda Bay (TX), 3, 5
Matson, 12, 60, 62, 63
McConnols, 56
Mercantilism, 7
Meridian Hall, 56
Miami, 29
Michilimackinac, 4, 9
Michimilimackinac, Straits of, 2
Millersburg, 115
Mineola, 36, 77, 78, 83
Missouri Fur Company, 17
Missouri Intelligencer, 37, 49, 102, 107
Missouri River, 6
Model T, 39
Moniteau Creek, 96, 103, 113
Montbrun's tavern, 19
Montgomery City, 74
Montgomery County, 51, 70-80
Montreal, 9

Mormons, 49
Morrison, James, 99, 110
Morrison, Jesse, 99, 110
Murry, 89
National Old Trails Road, 40, 69, 75, 79, 82, 84, 97, 103, 104, 113
Negro slaves. 11
New Franklin, 102, 105, 105, 113
New Madrid certificates, 22
New Madrid earthquakes, 22
New Madrid, 10
New Melle, 49, 55
New Mexico, 5, 39
New Orleans, 4, 5, 9
New Spain, 5, 7
Nicholas Coontz's Fort (also Kountz), 48
Nine Mile Prairie, 80, 81, 85
Niobrara River, 2
Nolan, Philip, 10
Nootka Bay, 9
North West Ordinance, 8
Northern Louisiana, 10
Ocean-to-Ocean Highway, 40
Ohio River, 8
Old Franklin, 99, 105, 106
Old Man Schaffer's Tavern, 48
Onate, Juan de, 32
Oregon Country, 39
Osage River, 20
Osage Trail, 14
Osage villages, 2
Osages (Indians), 24, 25, 28
Padoucas, 2
Parker, Oliver, 96, 97

Pawnees, 5
Peck, Charles and Ruloff, 46
Peck, John Mason, 50, 75, 86, 89, 90, 102
Pekitanoui, 2
Perche Creek, 91, 92, 115
Persia, 91, 92, 93
Peru, 7
Peruque Creek, 13, 14, 54, 68
Petersburg, 108, 109
Pike, Zebulon, 16, 19
Pinckney's Treaty, 8, 10
Pirogues, 58
Pitman Bridge, 51, 53
Pitman, John, 51
Plank roads, 39
Plat maps, 34
Platte River, 2, 5, 21
Point Labadie, 19
Polly, Mr., 82
Pond Fort, 15, 29, 52, 54, 68, 76
Pond, 14
Population density, 38
Portage des Sioux, 24, 31
Pottawattamie, 29
Prairie de Chien, 2, 4
Pre-emption, 22
Price, Gen. Sterling, 72
Price, Mr., 70
Principal meridians, 25, 27
Pringle, Norman, 56, 68
Quebec, 13
Ramsey family, 31
Range, 27, 32
Rector, William, 32, 33

Revolutionary War, 9
Roche persee, 20
Rocheport, 37, 84, 97, 113, 114
Roger Taylor;s Tavern, 68
Rothwell, Dan, 55, 70, 95
Royal Ordinance of 1736, 8
Rutgers, Arend, 13
Salt Creek Church, 104, 104
Salt Creek, 100, 109
Salt lick, 16
San Andres, 60
San Antonio, 5
San Carlos, 10
Sanborn Map, 43
Sanders Tavern, 69
Santa Fe Trail, 39, 40, 100, 102, 107
Sapp, David, 89, 94
Sauk (Indians), 60
Sauk, 24, 25, 29
Section line, 33
Section, 27, 34
Sexton's Tavern and road, 92
Slaves, 38
Smithton Company, 96
Smithton, 85, 115
Soulard Map, 23
Soulard, Antoine, 24
Spencer, George, 13
St Charles, 1, 12, 13, 14, 16, 17, 24, 29, 32, 33, 36, 37, 39, 41-49, 42, 49, 51, 57, 69, 72, 76, 78, 84, 85, 95
St. Charles County, 33, 41-56
St. Charles Street, 37, 92
St. Louis Enquirer, 37
St. Louis, 6, 21, 27, 37, 38, 41, 76, 77
St. Vrain, Jacques, 22
Ste, Genevieve, 8, 10
Steamboat Arabia, 107
Steamboat Independence, 38
Steamboats, 39
Tennessee, 8, 10
The Boonslick, 109
Thrall's Prairie, 95, 98
Thrall's Tavern, 96, 97
Three notched road, 55
Township, 32-34
Townships, 26, 27
Tract maps, 24
Treaty of Ghent. 31
Treaty of Paris, 5
Treaty of Tordesillas, 9
Trudeau, 11
Two Mile Prairie, 86, 89
Upper Louisiana, 11, 21, 57, 58
US Rangers, 28
Valverde, 5
Van Bibber Tavern, 34, 79, 80
Van Bibber, Isaac, 36, 78
Van Bibber, James, 61
Van Bibbers, 11, 58
Van Horn Tavern, 114, 115
Vancouver Island, 9
Viles, Jonas, 12, 37, 101
Villasur, 5
Vincennes, 4, 8
Virginia, 12, 76
Vivions Stage Stand, 115
Walker, Mr., 82
War of 1812, 9, 16, 24, 28, 50, 52,

54, 56, 60, 101
Ward, Mr., 85, 86
Warren County, 14, 33, 56, 67-70, 68
Warrenton, 68, 69
Wentzville, 40
Wessel Park, 64
Western House, 44
Western Plank Road, 51, 52
Westminster College, 116
Whetstone Creek, 81, 85, 86
Wilkinson, James, 9, 10, 110
Williamsburg, 37, 69, 80, 82, 83, 84, 94, 95
Williamson, Mr., 78
Windell, Marie George, 68
Winnebago, 29
Zumwalts, 13

www.ingramcontent.com/pod-product-compliance
Lightning Source LLC
Chambersburg PA
CBHW080249170426
43192CB00014BA/2614